DEVELOPMENT, GLOBALISATION AND SUSTAINABILITY

John Morgan

D1434504

Series Editor
Michael Witherick

Published in 2001 by:
Nelson Thornes Ltd
Delta Place
27 Bath Road
CHELTENHAM
GL53 7TH
United Kingdom

07 08 09 10 / 10 9 8 7 6 5

A catalogue record for this book is available from the British Library

ISBN 978 0 7487 5822 7

Illustrations and page make-up by Multiplex Techniques Ltd

Printed and bound in Slovenia by DELO tiskarna
by arrangement with Korotan Ljubljana

Acknowledgements
With thanks to the following for permission to reproduce photographs and other copyright material in this book:

Phillip Allen Publishing: *Geography Review*, March 2000, fig 1.2; Longman: *Geography and Development* R. Potter (1999), fig 1.4; Corbis/David Turnley: fig 4.7; Corel: figs 3.2, 3.3; Digital Vision: figs 3.1, 4.11.

Every effort has been made to contact copyright holders. The publishers apologise to anyone whose rights have been inadvertently overlooked, and will be happy to rectify any errors or omissions.

Contents

1

The nature of development

The development of development

The concept of development is complex and there are intense arguments about its meaning. Here are three dictionary definitions:

Some definitions of development

The act or process of developing: the state of being developed: a gradual unfolding or growth: evolution .... Advancing through successive stages to a higher, more complex, or more fully grown state.

Chambers English Dictionary

A process of becoming and a potential state of being. The achievement of a state of development would enable people in societies to make their own histories and geographies under conditions of their own choosing. The process of development is the means by which such conditions of human existence might be achieved.

Dictionary of Human Geography

The process by which some system, place, object or person is changed from one state into another; the term carries the connotation that the change is in the direction of growth or improvement.

Collins Reference Dictionary of Environmental Science

While there is a general awareness that 'development' is a positive thing (no one wants to be 'undeveloped'), it was not until about 1950 that most people in the richer countries began to accept that poorer countries could and should be developed, or that they were already developing. In the first half of the 20th century, it was widely believed that poor countries were meant to be poor. Countries in Asia and Africa were not thought to be capable of economic growth or progress, either because they had difficult climates (that is, tropical) or because they were populated by racial groups who lacked the skills of white people. Indeed, the discipline of geography spent a lot of time and effort seeking to demonstrate the 'inferiority' of non-white racial groups!

The new political context after the Second World War (1939–45) changed all this. The rise of Japan as an economic power and the process of de-colonisation were accompanied by a heightened optimism about the possibilities for development. Newly independent countries joined the United Nations (UN). The UN designated the 1960s as the 'Development Decade', and it was assumed that the development problems of the latecomer countries could be overcome through finance, technology and expertise from the developed countries, such as the USA and Britain. In 1966, the UN founded its Development Programme (UNDP), which is its principal development planning and coordinating body. It was in this period of optimism and global co-operation that Development Studies emerged as an academic discipline. Students taking these courses were taught to believe that a combination of economic planning in the countries of the developing world, plus foreign aid and investment from developed countries, would transform 'backward' traditional societies into modern industrial societies. In sum, the period after the Second World War was marked by the **ideology of developmentalism**; that is, by the belief that the countries of the world were on a path of inexorable progress and development.

By the 1970s, however, the optimism of the preceding Development Decade was being replaced by a growing awareness that inequalities between and within countries had actually worsened. Many developing countries had achieved economic growth as measured by Gross National Product (GNP), but this development was not equally shared amongst all the people. The third UN 'Development Decade' – the 1980s – was marked by a recognition that any attempt at development should take into account issues of distribution and of who gains from development. Economic growth was not enough, and measures needed to be taken to ensure that the benefits of such growth did not just fall to a small minority of the population. The 1980s also saw the gradual recognition that development needed to be sustainable; that it should take care to conserve natural resources and respect the environment. Despite these gains in the understanding of what development means, the 1980s are often referred to as the 'lost decade' in development terms. Apart from some notable exceptions, such as the newly industrialising countries (NICs), the majority of nations in the developing world actually experienced **development reversals** in the 1980s. In part, this can be explained by the onset of world recession in the early 1980s and the growing 'Third World' debt crisis.

The origins and effects of the debt crisis are complex. In attempting to reduce inflation rates, the Organisation for Economic Co-operation and Development (OECD) countries slowed down their economies, and this led to depressed prices and a reduced demand for commodities, which allowed interest rates to rise. For those developing countries that relied either on exporting or on borrowing as a source of foreign exchange, the results were disastrous. Higher interest rates meant that they had to pay out more and more to service their debts, and lower commodity prices meant that they received less revenue for their exports. In addition, commercial banks stopped lending them more money. The result was the debt crisis of the 1980s.

While the OECD countries recovered somewhat in the later part of the decade, the situation did not significantly improve for the developing countries. Continued high interest rates, along with reduced lending from banks, meant that many of them were paying out more in interest repayments than they received in borrowing. In addition, investment by foreign firms declined by nearly two-thirds in the 1980s; and the countries of the developed world adopted policies of protectionism, which made it more difficult for developing countries to export goods to them.

The effects of the 'lost decade' on the poorer countries were profound. GNP per capita actually declined in Latin America and Africa, along with investment. This meant that the infrastructure of transport, communications, education and health care worsened, and unemployment and underemployment grew.

Review

1 Attempt to write your own definition of **development**.

2 Explain what you understand by the **ideology of developmentalism**.

3 By means of an annotated sketch diagram, summarise how ideas about development have changed since the beginning of the 1960s.

4 Explain why the debt crisis is regarded as a major obstacle to development in many countries.

SECTION B

Measuring development

While reading the previous section, you may have wondered how a complex process such as development can be measured. There is no easy answer to that question. Indeed, geographers have spent a lot of time and energy wondering how to measure development. In a world in which decisions have to be made about allocating resources and deciding upon priorities for spending, it is increasingly important to have accurate and up-to-date information. However, there is no universally agreed measure of development. This section considers a number of attempts at measurement.

A common measurement of development is GNP (**1.1**). It is a measure of all of the goods and services produced by a country's population, both within its borders and abroad. The total figure is usually divided by the country's population to arrive at a per capita value, which makes it possible to compare the average income of different countries. GNP has been described as a 'grotesque' measure of development. This is because it tends to be expressed as a 'per capita' measure and therefore does not take into account the distribution of wealth within a population. Also, it tends to include things that are recognised as social 'ills'. For example, cleaning up the environment after an oil-spill counts towards GNP.

An alternative measure of development is the Human Development Index (HDI) devised by the UNDP for its annual *Human Development Report* (**1.2**). It yields a result of between 0 and 1. It has the advantages of:

■ being easy to understand
■ providing a basis for ranking of countries
■ enabling comparisons of the performance of a country over time.

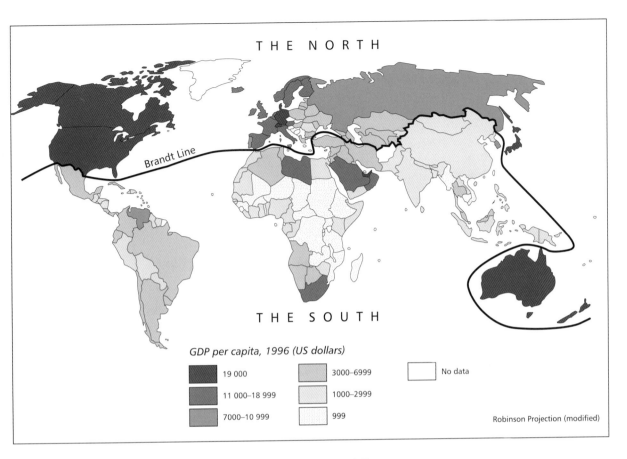

THE NORTH

Brandt Line

THE SOUTH

GDP per capita, 1996 (US dollars)

19 000	3000–6999	No data
11 000–18 999	1000–2999	
7000–10 999	999	

Robinson Projection (modified)

Figure 1.1 The global distribution of per capita GNP

The HDI can be calculated as follows:

Calculating the HDI

The Human Development Index (HDI) for any country is calculated using three variables:

- income – measured by GDP per capita
- knowledge – measured by adult literacy and the percentage of children attending school
- longevity – measured by life expectancy at birth.

For each variable, the highest and lowest values for all of the world's countries are found. The highest possible measure is awarded a score of 1, and the lowest 0. Each country can then be assessed against this scale. For example, the highest life expectancy is 80 years, in Japan, and the lowest is 37, in Senegal. A country with a life expectancy halfway between 80 and 37 would be given a score of 0.5. The scores for each of the three variables are averaged out to give the total HDI.

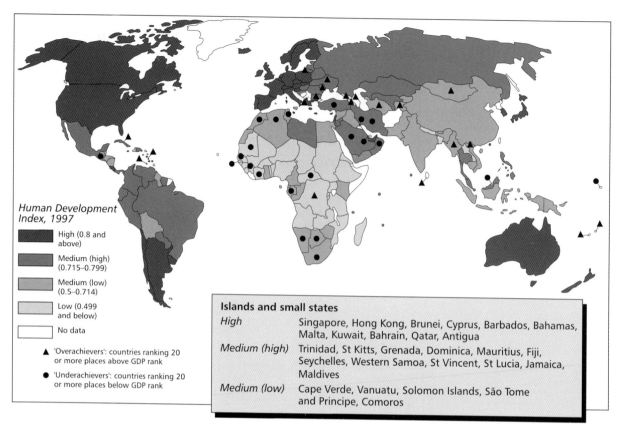

Human Development
Index, 1997

High (0.8 and above)

Medium (high) (0.715–0.799)

Medium (low) (0.5–0.714)

Low (0.499 and below)

No data

▲ 'Overachievers': countries ranking 20 or more places above GDP rank

● 'Underachievers': countries ranking 20 or more places below GDP rank

Islands and small states

High	Singapore, Hong Kong, Brunei, Cyprus, Barbados, Bahamas, Malta, Kuwait, Bahrain, Qatar, Antigua
Medium (high)	Trinidad, St Kitts, Grenada, Dominica, Mauritius, Fiji, Seychelles, Western Samoa, St Vincent, St Lucia, Jamaica, Maldives
Medium (low)	Cape Verde, Vanuatu, Solomon Islands, São Tome and Principe, Comoros

Figure 1.2 The global distribution of the HDI value

This aggregate measure has a number of advantages. Alistair Rogers (2000) provides a useful summary of what the HDI shows:

> *Countries which rank lower may be called 'underachievers'. They often have productive economies, but have not converted their wealth into longer lives or better education ... many oil-rich countries in the Middle East and North Africa fall into this category. In many cases they have low levels of female education, strong income inequality and large migrant communities without human rights.*

> *Then again, some countries have done remarkably well in using modest amounts of wealth to improve the lot of their citizens. These 'overachievers' include many formerly socialist countries such as Ukraine and Lithuania, and small island states such as Dominica and Fiji.*

The UNDP has also established a development index to measure the status of women. This is based on employment levels, wage rates, adult literacy, years of schooling and life expectancy. The gender index raises some important issues. According to the index, in no country are women as a group better off than men. In many developed countries, the score for women is between 85 and 95 per cent of the score for men. Japan, ranked fourth on its HDI score, is ranked eighth on the gender-related development index, because Japanese women have lower employment and wage rates than men. The most noticeable differences are between developed and developing countries. In much of Africa and Latin America, the scores for women are only between 55 and 65 per cent of those for men.

The measurements of development discussed so far are all generalised measures that deal in averages and aggregate data. While they provide a general indication of levels of development, they can have the effect of obscuring the nature and causes of development. They also tend to conceal geographical and social variations and inequalities. Finally, these measures rely on official data – and the accuracy of that data is not always assured.

All this talk of aggregate statistics and indices of development can obscure the reality of what concepts such as 'development' and 'underdevelopment' actually mean. The following passage was written in 1963 by Robert Heilbroner, and was an attempt to demonstrate to a North American audience what underdevelopment might actually mean to a typical US family:

> We begin by invading the house ... to strip it of its furniture. Everything goes: beds, chairs, tables, television set, lamps. We will leave the family with a few old blankets, a kitchen table, a wooden chair. Along with the bureaus go the clothes. Each member of the family may keep in their 'wardrobe' their oldest suit or dress, a shirt or blouse. We will permit a pair of shoes to the head of the family, but none for the wife or children.
>
> We move to the kitchen. The appliances have already been taken out, so we turn to the cupboards and larder. The box of matches may stay, a small bag of flour, some sugar and salt. A few mouldy potatoes, already in the garbage can, must be hastily rescued, for they will provide much of tonight's meal ...
>
> Now we have stripped the house: the bathroom has been dismantled, the running water switched off, the electric wires taken out. Next we take away the house. The family can move to the tool shed. It is crowded, but much better than the situation in Hong Kong ...
>
> But we have only begun. All the other houses in the neighbourhood have also been removed; our suburb has become a shanty town. Still, our family is lucky to have shelter ...
>
> Communications must go next. No more newspapers, magazines, books – not that they are missed, since we must take away our family's literacy as well. Instead, in our shanty town we will allow one radio.
>
> Now government services must go. No more postman, no more fireman. There is a school, but it is three miles away and consists of two classrooms ... There are, of course, no hospitals or doctors nearby. The nearest clinic is ten miles away ...
>
> Of course, this is only an impression of life in the underdeveloped lands. It is not life itself. Still lacking are those things that underdevelopment gives as well as those that it takes away: the urinous smell of poverty, the display of disease, the flies, the open sewers.
>
> [But when] we are told that half the world's population enjoys a standard of living 'less than $100 a year', this is what the figures mean.

Review

5 Distinguish between GDP and GNP.

6 Discuss the value of per capita GNP as a measure of development.

7 What do you see as the particular merits of the HDI?

8 Study **1.1** and **1.2**. Describe and compare the main features of their distribution patterns.

A word of caution about terminology

In any book dealing with the topic of development, the thorny question of terminology has to be addressed. Language is important, and the terms used change their meaning over time. For example, when the author went to school, back in the late 1970s, he came across geography textbooks that used the term 'backward' to describe some countries in Africa and Asia. Such a term would not be acceptable today. The modern use of the word 'development' comes from the US President Harry S. Truman's comment in 1949, that the underdeveloped world's poverty is

> *a handicap and a threat both to them and more prosperous areas …
> greater production is the key to prosperity and peace.*

There is a good deal of controversy over the use of the term 'underdeveloped'. Some people favour the term 'developing', to highlight the fact that development is a process rather than a fixed state, while others prefer to preface the word developed with either 'more' or 'less'. Indeed, some examination boards use the terms More Economically Developed Countries (MEDCs) and Less Economically Developed Countries (LEDCs), presumably to suggest that although some countries may not have such high GNP per capita, this should not imply that they are socially, culturally or politically inferior.

Another term that presents difficulty is 'Third World'. This is often used as a shorthand for poverty, but its origins are political – it represents countries searching for an alternative to the communist or fascist regimes that dominated European politics in the 1930s. In his book *Third World*, the sociologist Peter Worsley used the term to describe a group of nations with a colonial past from which they have recently escaped. More commonly, the term is used as a shorthand to refer to the developing world.

The Brandt Report of 1981 set up an opposition between the rich and poor worlds – the developed and underdeveloped worlds – through the use of the terms North and South (**1.1**). From the strictly geographical point of view, the line proposed by Brandt is inaccurate. The South includes many states in the Northern Hemisphere, such as China, whereas Australasia comprises part of the North.

One final example that demonstrates the way in which the choice of terminology is never neutral is the distinction between the Minority World and the Majority World. The Majority World has the greatest proportion of the world's population and the largest land mass, compared to the smaller size of the Minority World. The use of the term reminds us that people who live in the Minority World tend to experience more privileged lifestyles compared with the population of the Majority World. Terms such as 'developing', 'less-developed', 'low-income' and 'undeveloped' tend to emphasise what such countries lack, while the terms 'Majority World' and 'Minority World' shift the balance, so that the richer countries are defined in terms of what they lack. The use of these terms attempts to prompt the reader to pause and reflect on the unequal relations between the rich and poor.

This discussion of the terms used to describe the state of development highlights the need to be aware of the importance of language. It suggests that, however neutral or scientific we may try to be in writing geographical accounts, such terms always reflect values and beliefs about the nature of the world. For example, to claim to be neutral or unbiased is to adopt certain values or beliefs about what is good. There is probably no solution to this. In this book, the terms generally used are 'developed' and 'developing' countries.

Review

9 Make of list of the pairings of terms used to describe the two major divisions of the world as regards the level of development. Make critical comments about each pairing. Which pairing do you prefer? Give your reasons.

SECTION D

Approaches to development

The first few pages of this book have hopefully persuaded you that, when it comes to discussing development, nothing is straightforward. How we define development, how we measure it and even the terms that we use are the subject of argument and debate. This is not something to bemoan, although it does mean that your work as an A-level geography student is more complicated. Indeed, it is probably the case that the more hotly contested a concept is, the more likely it is that it describes something important.

In the remainder of this chapter, we discuss the theories and models that have been put forward to explain development. In doing so, we need to be aware that there are at least two different viewpoints, which relate to where you live on the globe.

The view from the developed world

Modernisation theories of development are based on the idea that all nations occupy positions on a continuum, that runs from traditional societies at one extreme to modern societies at the other. Countries can move from 'traditional' to 'modern' by adopting the characteristics of modern societies. Perhaps the most influential example of this type of theory is that of the economic historian W. W. Rostow. He postulated that there were five stages through which all countries have to pass in the development process: the traditional society, preconditions for take-off, take-off, the drive to maturity and the age of mass consumption (**1.3**). Rostow was suggesting that higher levels of consumer demand, entrepreneurship and increased technical knowledge drive the economy to higher levels of economic growth.

Case study: Rostow's five-stage model of development

Figure 1.3 Rostow's five-stage model of development

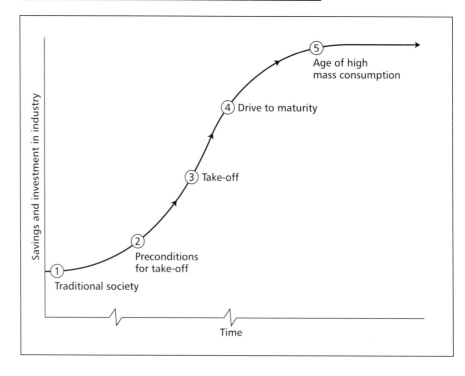

Stage 1: traditional society
Production is limited and productivity is low. Society is heavily dependent on agriculture, and there is a reliance on pre-scientific modes of knowledge. The social and political systems tend to be feudal and hierarchical, and there tends to be a strong element of fatalism in the belief system of the society.

Stage 2: preconditions for take-off
Although productivity is still low, the insights of modern science are translated into new production methods in agriculture and industry. These developments often come from external influences such as colonisation, which shake traditional value systems and introduce the idea of economic progress as a public good.

Stage 3: take-off
This is the vital 'watershed' in the development of modern societies. The important spur is an increase in the level of savings that facilitates an increase in the level of economic investment. New production methods are developed, while the agricultural sector is mechanised and shifts from a subsistence to a commercial mode. An expanding class of capitalists and entrepreneurs emerges.

Stage 4: the drive to maturity
In the long period after 'take-off', modern technology spreads over the whole of economic production. Investment levels are high, and output of goods and services increases faster than the rate of population increase, thus leading to higher per capita income. The nation begins to specialise in certain goods and contributes to international trade.

Stage 5: the age of high mass consumption
In this last stage, the leading economic sectors are to do with durable consumer goods and services. Real income rises to a level that allows people to consume at levels far above their basic needs for food and shelter. In this stage, questions of quality of life become important, and the goal of society is no longer simply about increasing levels of economic production.

Rostow's model was most popular in the 1960s. This was a period during which the economic boom that followed the Second World War seemed to provide the hope of prosperity for all countries. The model reflected the ideology of developmentalism, or the belief that the nations of the world were following the slow but inevitable path to Western prosperity. It has also been criticised for its Eurocentricity, since it appears to suggest that all countries will follow the same path as countries in Europe and North America. However, as the economic crises of the late 1960s and early 1970s developed, the model became less fashionable, and it was challenged by theories of the core and the periphery. It is to these theories that we now turn.

Core–periphery models of development are associated with the work of Gunnar Myrdal, Albert Hirschman and John Friedmann. These writers were concerned with the way in which developing countries were becoming increasingly divided into a growing 'modern' **core** region linked to the international economy and a stagnating 'traditional' **periphery**. The crux of their argument was that an assumption in modernisation theory – that development would lead to the gradual elimination of geographical differences in levels of economic development – was flawed. They pointed out that the 'multiplier effects' of an investment tend to be limited to local areas and do not easily **trickle down** to other locations. Myrdal's concept of **cumulative causation** captures this idea. He argued that, instead of the trickle-down or **spread effect**, there is a **backwash effect** whereby a wealthy region attracts migrants, capital and investment. The overall effect is the gradual widening of inequalities between regions. Hirschman and Friedman developed similar arguments, but were more optimistic that ways could be found to overcome these imbalances. For example, this might be achieved by concentrating investment in the peripheral regions and then relying on the associated local multiplier effect to stimulate growth.

The Swedish economist Gunnar Myrdal (1956) argued that regional differences are the natural outcome of economic development. The increased prosperity of one region inevitably affects the prosperity of another. Economic development is triggered by the availability of resources such as fuel or raw materials. Once set in motion, it leads to a process of cumulative causation. Capital in the form of investment and labour is attracted into the expanding area, which drains surrounding areas of investment and workers. At the same time, through the multiplier effect, growing industries lead to the development of other industries. This chain reaction produces a **virtuous cycle** of economic growth. Myrdal called the movement of wealth from the poorer to the richer regions the **backwash effect**. Eventually, he suggested, the increased wealth in the developed region would percolate or **trickle down** to the less-developed region. This was called the **spread effect** (1.4).

Figure 1.4 To what extent is the development of the developed countries 'propped up' by developing countries?

The North American economist Albert Hirschman (1958) produced conclusions that were similar to those of Myrdal. He described the growth of the **core**, which resulted from **virtuous circles** or **upward spirals** of development; and the stagnation of the **periphery**, due to it being impeded by **vicious circles** or **downward spirals** of underdevelopment. The main difference between Myrdal and Hirschman is that latter was more optimistic about the extent to which the polarisation between the core and the periphery could be overcome.

It is sometimes easy to become overwhelmed by all the different theories offered about development. This is especially so because it is not easy to gain empirical evidence with which to assess their value. Geographers increasingly recognise that all theories reflect the social and geographical locations of those who have produced them. In the case of the theories discussed so far, the locations of the different theorists are quite similar. They all write from academic, male and middle-class experiences and, most importantly, from a developed-world perspective. Development looks very different from those places that are in the process of experiencing it. It to this perspective that we now turn.

The view from the developing world

From the 1960s onwards, writers from the so-called 'Third World', or less-developed world, have sought to challenge the development theories produced by Western academics. **Dependency theories** of development suggest that the links between developed and less-developed countries are actually the cause of worsening conditions in the developing world. Rather than seeing underdevelopment as a 'natural' and inevitable condition, it is viewed as a consequence of the way in which the world economy works. This 'development of underdevelopment' perspective opposes the view of development that is favoured by modernisation theory.

One of the most influential models of dependency theory was proposed by Andre Gunder Frank. Writing in the late 1960s, he argued that since Latin America was discovered by Europeans, it has inevitably had a capitalist market economy geared to trade with Europe and North America. Such trade has always been unequal because of Latin America's very dependence upon it. The fact that Latin America is underdeveloped is seen, therefore, as a consequence of its involvement in capitalist trade. The elite groups within Latin American countries have acted in the interests of capitalists in Europe and North America, and have been rewarded with relative wealth and power. The outcome is a dual society in Latin America, divided between the rich and the poor.

Closely linked to dependency theory is **world systems theory**, which is associated with the work of Immanuel Wallerstein and Samir Amin. This theory seeks to explain the state of development of any nation in terms of its position in a interconnected capitalist world economy. Amin argued that the expansion of capitalist production in Europe and North America required large amounts of raw materials from the less-developed world. The pre-capitalist forms of production in these countries meant that these raw materials could be obtained while workers were paid low wages. In this way, countries in the less-developed world were involved in supplying raw materials, while the developed countries processed them into finished goods. Amin called the former the 'periphery' and the latter the 'core'. As a result of these two functions, the core countries become wealthy and the peripheral countries remain poor. Because workers in the peripheral countries receive lower wages, so the demand for consumer goods there remains small. This in turn means that investment in production remains limited. Amin concluded that unequal development between the core and periphery is, and will continue to be, the rule.

It is important to understand the context in which views stressing the development of underdevelopment were formulated. Writers such as Frank and Amin were deliberately opposing the theories of modernisation proposed by theorists in the developed world. They wanted to show that a nation's position in the world system as a whole would influence its development path. They were opposed to what has been called the 'error of developmentalism', which assumed (as did Rostow) that all societies would follow the same pathway to development.

From the account offered so far, we can see that developed-world perspectives on development were challenged in the 1970s and early 1980s from less-developed world dependency perspectives. Such perspectives have themselves been the subject of intense debate within the field of development studies. Finally in this chapter, we bring the story up to date by looking at some of the current arguments about development. Hopefully, it will be clear by now that all theories must be viewed in their context, and we need to ask not just who is producing them but, more importantly, where and why.

Review

10 Check that you understand the main features of modernisation theory.

11 Summarise the main features of Rostow's model, pointing out its strengths and weaknesses.

12 Identify the essential features of dependency theory.

Recent debates

The 1980s and 1990s witnessed the emergence of a new school of modernisation studies. This school argues that there is more than one path towards development. Instead of seeing the distinct cultural characteristics of countries as obstacles to development that need to be overcome, it is argued that development must be sensitive to the specific conditions that exist in a country. However, while it is recognised that the societies will differ in their development pathways, it is assumed that the goal of development will be to achieve developed-world economic standards of wealth and prosperity. In other words, standard economic measures remain the indicators of successful development. Critics of this view suggest that these theories are being used to justify the policies of organisations such as the World Bank and the International Monetary Fund. These global organisations have a particular view of development which involves:

- increasing trade
- encouraging economic growth
- cutting back public spending on services such as health and education, in favour of privatisation.

Critics suggest that this view is little more than the revival of Rostow's stages of growth theory in a modern, updated form.

A second set of ideas that influences current debates about development is that associated with **sustainable development**, which was defined in the Bruntland Report of 1987 as 'development which meets the needs of the present without compromising the ability of future generations to meet their own needs'. We will consider sustainability in detail later, in **Chapter 6**. For the moment, it is important to recognise that the challenge that it presents is whether, in the context of development, economic goals should take priority over environmental goals. There are important issues here, not least of which is the extent to which sustainable development is being promoted by powerful countries in the developed world as a model to be followed by countries in the less-developed world. As always, discussions about the best forms of development are linked to important political questions.

In contrast to these more recent ideas about the possibilities for development are those that have been labelled **anti-** or **post-development**. They emanate from the developing world, and argue that the very idea of development as material economic prosperity combined with the Western vision of democracy is itself Eurocentric. They point out that the overall effect of global capitalism and development strategies has been to eliminate alternative visions of development. Development as the 'catching up with the West' has the result of disempowering less-developed world people. First, it convinces people that their own knowledge, values, institutions and cultures are less 'developed' than those of people in the West. Second, although 'development' can be an innocent word expressing the best of intentions, in fact it is mainly used to justify the intervention by the 'more developed' in the lives of those considered to be 'underdeveloped'. The task of deciding on the means of development has been taken to be a technical task, to be handled by professionals and organisations that are qualified to carry out such a complex task as development. The knowledge of ordinary people is considered to be subjective and value-laden. Anti-developmentalism argues that development reflects ways of thinking that are Eurocentric, middle-class and masculine, and that favour powerful political and economic interests.

Another aspect of the argument against development is that development thinking produces and justifies certain types of policy, programme and project. While they often increase the flow of goods and services to the upper middle and middle classes, at the same time they:

- create scarcity among other groups
- degrade the environment
- undermine the physical and cultural support systems of poorer groups.

At the heart of development thinking is the idea that rapid growth in GNP is the key to development. However, it is pointed out that 'invisible' categories are ignored in this approach. For example, take the case of self-provisioning, where people eat home-grown food, live in self-built houses or wear home-made clothes. From the point of view of development, these resources are considered to be 'under-utilised', because they have not been turned into commodities for sale on the market.

Arturo Escobar is the writer most closely associated with the idea of post-developmentalism. While writers such as Frank and Amin advocated socialism as a pathway to development, Escobar goes further and condemns the idea of development itself. He claims that it is responsible for 'discovering' mass poverty, and for promoting the illusion of social improvement by means of European models of economic change and advancement. He dates the invention of development to that speech by US President Harry S. Truman in 1949, quoted on page 10. In this speech, the 'underdeveloped areas' of the globe were described as suffering from disease and inadequate food supplies. Truman proposed that the USA and its richer allies should fund a 'program of development'. Escobar refuses to see this 'fair deal' as a gesture of innocent goodwill. He asks why it was that the developed countries came to define themselves in opposition to the 'underdeveloped countries' and demanded that the latter be remade in the image of the former. He identifies a Western mind-set that defines the less-developed world as a place of poverty, disease and deprivation, which needs to be fixed by doses of Western capital and know-how. These projects to develop the 'Third World' are ignorant of the expressed needs and knowledge of local people. The result is a nightmare for those who are subjected to development.

A good example of the argument about the detrimental effects of development is provided by the Green Revolution, in which the hybrid seeds developed by developed-world scientists were intended to improve less-developed world food production. On a purely technical level, the new seeds produce higher grain yields when they are used according to the manufacturers' instructions. However, the use of the new high-yielding varieties also involves the diffusion of a new culture. This culture tends to place less stress on the importance of subsistence and the principle of local production. Instead, the new seeds represent the imposition of Western science, capital and authority, which take precedence over traditional ways of using the land and the knowledge on which that is based. Government then assumes responsibility for agricultural improvement while failing to improve other forms of food production. The point of this example is that while technology can lead to development, we need to think more carefully about the nature of that development.

As we enter a new millennium, then, the idea of development remains a hotly contested one. Within geography, there is a concern that development is closely linked to the idea of modernity. According to this view, development is concerned with providing a single over-arching solution to the problems of people in the developing world. Modernism is based on the idea that development is all about transforming traditional countries into modern, Westernised ones. This tends to ignore the idea that people in traditional societies might be perfectly content, and might have equally valid ways of life. Figure **1.5** highlights the differences between the pro-development and anti-development arguments.

Figure 1.5 Opposing views of development

Pro-development	Anti-development
Development leads to economic growth	Development is a dependent and subordinating process; it is something done by the powerful to the less powerful
Development brings overall national progress	Development creates and widens spatial inequalities
Development leads to modernisation along Western lines	Development undermines local cultures and ways of life
Development improves the provision of basic needs	Development perpetuates poverty and poor working and living conditions
Development can lead to sustainable growth	Development is often environmentally unsustainable
Development leads to the improved management of people and the environment	Development infringes human rights and undermines democracy

Review

13 Study **1.5**. Which set of arguments do you find more convincing? Give your reasons.

14 'The Green Revolution has had a mixed reception.' Explain what is meant by this statement.

SECTION F

Review

15 'Where you live colours your view of development.' Discuss.

16 What might happen to a country if it were to adopt an anti-development policy? Are there any real alternatives to development?

Conclusions

This chapter has deliberately raised important questions about the nature of development. It has attempted to highlight the fact that development is a concept that is open to a range of interpretations. An important part of this argument is that the types of theory about development that litter the pages of school geography textbooks have to be seen as offering particular perspectives on development. We have stressed the difference between modernisation theories produced, by and large, by people in the developed countries of the world and dependency theories produced by people in the developing countries. In addition, attention has been drawn to the view in geography that development as a concept is inextricably linked to powerful ideas about the superiority of the West and its forms of science and economy. In opposition to this, anti-development or post-development theories argue for the positive valuation of the traditional ways of life and knowledge of people in the developing world. These ideas are not easy, not least because they are largely unfamiliar to those of us who are brought up with a developed-world perspective.

Enquiry

Select a range of geography textbooks that deal with the issue of 'development'. Read their sections on development.

a Which models and theories do they use to explain development?
b Do the models and theories largely reflect Western viewpoints on development, or do they incorporate alternative views?
c Is there any evidence of 'post-development' views in the textbooks that you have read?
d To what extent do you think textbooks should present a 'balanced view' of development issues?

2

A global world

Introduction

You may have noticed that the discussion of development in the previous chapter tended to make reference to individual countries or nations. We were talking about the levels of development of individual countries and the differences between them. In one sense, this is perfectly understandable, since a glance at an atlas or globe will confirm that the world is divided into political units. However, in another sense a focus on the scale of individual nations tends to deflect our attention from the fact that the boundaries between nations are artificial. All of us are part of a global totality.

In recent decades, this consciousness of the global scale has become particularly important, and we increasingly recognise the importance of analysing issues at a global scale. This is reflected in the work of geographers. For example, in their introduction to *A World in Crisis?*, the geographers Ronald Johnston and Peter Taylor commented that:

> *it is obvious to all but the most myopic of observers that the current changes have no respect for national boundaries; they are spread, albeit in different manifestations, across the whole face of the Earth, with states almost powerless to influence them. Hence we have global problems, a world recession, international stagnation ... perhaps even a world in crisis.*

In the years since this book was published (1986), the type of 'global thinking' that Johnston and Taylor described has become even more common, leading some people to reflect that **globalisation** has become the buzzword of the social sciences in the 1990s and beyond.

The extent to which the idea of globalisation has come to influence our thinking is indicated by the fact that the World Bank, in the 1995 edition of the *World Development Report*, stated that 'these are revolutionary times in the global economy'. The Report describes how globalisation affects the lives of three different people in three different places:

Profiles of three global citizens

Joe lives in a small town in southern Texas. His old job as an accounts clerk in a textile firm, where he had worked for many years, was not very secure. He earned $50 a day, but promises of promotion never came through, and the firm eventually went out of business as cheap imports from Mexico forced textile prices down. Joe went back to

---

college to study business administration and was recently hired by one of the new banks in the area. He enjoys a comfortable living even after making the monthly payments on his government-subsidised student loan.

Maria recently moved from her central Mexican village and now works in a US-owned firm in Mexico's maquiladora sector. Her husband, Juan, runs a small car upholstery business and sometimes crosses the border during the harvest sector to work illegally on farms in California. Maria, Juan, and their son have improved their standard of living since moving out of subsistence agriculture, but Maria's wage has not increased in years: she still earns about $10 a day.

Xiao Zhi is an industrial worker in Shenzhen, a Special Economic Zone in China. After three difficult years on the road as part of China's floating population, fleeing from the poverty of nearby Sichuan province, he has finally settled with a new firm from Hong Kong that produces garments for the US market. He can afford more than a bowl of rice for his daily meal. He makes $2 a day and is hopeful for his future.

Workers in the developed world, such as Joe, lose their jobs because of competition from poor Mexicans like Maria, whose wages are in turn held down by cheaper imports from China. But these changes also bring with them new geographies of opportunities. Joe was able to retrain and take up work in the expanding quaternary sector, and the growth of US exports to Mexico has meant that Maria has an improved standard of living, and that her son can imagine a better future. Xiao is looking forward to higher wages and the prospect of buying consumer goods. However, this story has a darker side. It has to be pointed out that not everyone benefits from these changes in the global economy. Workers face a future in which there is insecurity about their future employment, and workers fear that they may lose their jobs as firms relocate to countries in which wages are lower. The gap between the rich and the poor is widening, and many people – such as those, unlike Xiao Zhi, who are left in the Chinese countryside – are excluded from sharing the benefits of globalisation.

This chapter has three major aims:

- to distinguish between economic, political and cultural globalisation
- to provide an outline history of these processes, particularly the first
- to identify the causes of economic globalisation.

Review

1 Explain what the three portraits in the above panel tell us about globalisation.

Globalisation

It was Karl Marx who first spoke of the role of communications technologies in leading to the 'annihilation of space by time', as goods were exchanged over greater and greater distances. Marshall McLuhan used the term **global village** to capture the idea that the world was becoming 'compressed' and electronically connected, so that 'the global is no more than a village'. Writing from a developed country such as the UK, it is easy to think of examples of globalisation and understand its impacts on our daily lives. To begin with, many of you who are reading this book will have taken a holiday that has involved international travel and – given that some of you will go to universities and gain degrees – many of you will, in the future, join that segment of the population that has access to regular travel. From such a perspective, it is easy to grasp the idea that the world is shrinking in terms of the distance that can be travelled in a given time period. Apart from physical travel, we feel more connected to other parts of the world, since developments in communications – such as satellite television – mean that we can hear about what is happening elsewhere more quickly than ever. Finally, we realise that certain products – such as a Big Mac or Coca-Cola – are available throughout the world (**2.1**).

Figure 2.1 McDonald's in Poland – does the globalisation of food signal the arrival of a 'global diet'?

Geographers recognise that there are three broad strands to globalisation: the economic, the political and the cultural.

Economic globalisation

According to the theories of globalisation, the world economy has become 'globalised' through the growth of global production, global markets and global finance. Multinational firms roam the globe in search of new markets and places to locate production, leading to the shift in production from the developed to the developing world. These processes have been aided by the free flow of capital on a global scale, as barriers to investment have been removed. Direct investment across national borders has increased, which means that the economy operates on a global scale and is intensely competitive as countries seek to attract new investment.

At the heart of this process are transnational corporations (TNCs), which develop new strategies for improved profits through measures that make use of the international division of labour and production. The global flow of capital and ideas, at new speeds and over greater distances, is facilitated by advances in electronic communication (such as the Internet) and by the altered international regulation and operation of financial markets. The 'shrinking world' made possible by technological change enables TNCs to exploit wage differences between countries and regions, moving low-grade tasks to less-unionised and lower-paid locations, such as India or Jamaica. In turn, much of this labour force is made up of women, who constitute a supply of 'green' labour that is plentiful, cheap and apparently compliant. The extent to which production processes have become mobile and global markets increasingly connected all suggest that space may indeed have been annihilated.

At the continental level, the flow of money, goods and services is eased by new trading blocs such as the European Union (EU), the North American Free Trade Association (NAFTA) or the Southern Cone Common Market (Mercosur). As economic globalisation has developed, TNCs and banks have increased their significance in the world economy. Individual countries or nation–states have become less able to control the transactions that now cross their borders. At the same time, countries have become more entrepreneurial, seeking to attract new investment by competing with other states. They may do this by lowering taxes or offering other incentives to encourage inward investment. International organisations such as the Internal Monetary Fund (IMF), the World Bank and the World Trade Organisation (WTO) are all influential in promoting the idea of more open international trade and free markets.

On the other hand, enforced crossing of borders and displacement in the past 20 years has produced unprecedented numbers of refugees and asylum seekers, the majority of whom are women. The paradox is that as global population movements have increased, so has the drawing of boundaries and exclusions, as illustrated by the idea of the 'Fortress Europe' immigration policies of the EU.

Political globalisation

The processes of economic globalisation raise questions about the changing shape of political power. Some writers have claimed that the power and importance of the nation–state has been reduced, as individual states are now less able to determine their own policies. The crash of many South-East Asian economies in 1997/8 and the knock-on effects of these events on financial markets and job losses indicate this **de-territorialisation of power**. Others claim that the death of the nation–state is exaggerated and dispute any notion that 'geography is history' (as a recent British Telecom advert proclaimed). Instead, they say that states retain considerable influence in their policy decisions on a vast range of domestic issues, from the scale and form of service provision, to tax and welfare regimes and the shape of the political system itself.

Cultural globalisation

Globalisation is also is a cultural phenomenon. The idea of a global culture is made possible by communications technologies that circulate globalised popular cultures (for instance, the popular TV game show 'Who Wants to be a Millionaire?' is adapted to 85 countries worldwide). There has been an important debate about the extent to which globalisation promotes the homogeneity of culture and whether it creates an opportunity for the construction of new forms of hybrid cultures. Whatever the case, the ability to connect beyond the local may be a liberation or revelation for some, and may lead to a possible reworking of personal identities. It is worth remembering that new technologies are linked to uneven and unequal social relations, such as the overwhelming dominance of male producers and consumers of Information Technology (IT).

The globalisation of culture is not simply technologically driven. Other powerful forces are migration and diaspora. We live in an age of migration. Increasing numbers of migrants are paralleled by the globalisation of migration. More and more countries are becoming incorporated in wider systems of population movement. These are driven by processes of uneven development. These global population movements generate transnational linkages and 'stretched out' social relations. At the same time, those movements produce **diaspora**; namely, the dispersal across geographical and political boundaries of people who share the same cultural affiliations and identities. These processes lead to the emergence of hybrid cultures.

The globalising demand for the consumption of other cultures also arises from the opportunities for profit gained from the commodification of difference. Responses to these processes of change vary considerably. While in some places globalising cultural processes may be welcomed, in other cases the response may be the reassertion of local identification and a stress on more bounded notions of belonging – as, for example, in the current resurgence of racism and xenophobia in parts of Europe.

Review

2 Attempt a definition of **globalisation**.

3 Explain what is meant by, and give examples of, the terms **economic globalisation**, **political globalisation** and **cultural globalisation**.

A brief history of globalisation

Just as there are scholarly arguments about the existence and form of globalisation, so there are arguments about the development of globalisation. In this section, one account of the history of globalisation is outlined. It is possible to identify three phases of globalisation to date:

- the emergence of a global consciousness
- the spread of globalisation from the middle of the 19th century and its increase at a gradual rate for the next 100 years
- the proliferation of global relations since the 1960s.

The phase of incipient globalisation, 1850–1950

Although the roots of globalisation can be identified as having existed in earlier stages of human history, it was not until the 1850s that the means to take globalisation beyond the imagination developed. This relied on the development of communications technologies, global markets and global organisations. In terms of communications, the years from 1850 to 1950 were important in the evolution of new technologies. This period saw the emergence of the telegraph as the first means of global communication. For example, submarine telegraph became available in the early 1850s, and transatlantic cable was in permanent use by 1866. Five years later, telegraph lines stretched continuously from Europe to as far as China, Japan and Australia.

The late 19th century saw the telephone become a means of international communication. The first trans-border call between Paris and London was made in 1891, and by 1926 there were two-way telephone communications across the Atlantic. Indeed, by 1933 an advertisement for the American Telephone and Telegraph Company (AT&T) claimed that the 'world is bound together by telephone'. This period also saw the development of radio as a means of international communication. The first wireless transmission across the English Channel was made in 1899, and the BBC World Service was launched in 1924. Finally, the early 20th century witnessed the advent of mechanised air transport. Airmail services began in 1918, and the first non-stop transatlantic flight took place in 1919.

While the period from 1850 to 1950 saw the development of the means of global communication, it is worth remembering that before the 1960s, apart from radio, global communications were outside the experience of the vast majority of people – and that they were slow and expensive. For example, the cost of a telephone call from London to New York in 1927 was almost one thousand times greater in real terms than in 1996. Moreover, it was overwhelmingly the case that the technologies discussed here were only available in a few countries, such as the USA and the nations of Europe.

The development of communications technology in the period from 1850 to 1950 was accompanied by the establishment of global markets for certain products. For example, a prototypical global market in copper developed from the 1850s onwards, and the London Metal Exchange was established in 1876 to handle deals in copper, zinc, lead and tin. In addition, a global market for some packaged goods developed from the late 19th century. For instance, products such as Campbell's soup and Heinz foods became household articles from the mid-1880s, and Coca-Cola was marketed in Britain, Canada, Cuba, Mexico and the USA within 20 years of its introduction in 1886. The range of products marketed globally continued to grow in the early 20th century with, for example, the international marketing of Bayer aspirin and Gillette razors. In 1908, Ford's Model T was envisaged as a 'world car'. By 1929, Coca-Cola was bottled in 27 countries and sold in 78. The Marlboro cowboy appeared in 1954 and the first McDonald's opened in 1955. These examples give a sense of the development of an emerging global market in this period.

The phase of incipient globalisation also saw the emergence of a range of organisations that operated on a global scale. A number of those companies have already been mentioned. Many began to develop enterprises in other countries. For instance, the US gun-maker Colt opened a factory in Britain in 1852, the German-based Siemens built a production facility in Russia in 1855, and Kikkoman of Japan set up soy sauce manufacture in the USA in 1852.

Other organisations formed during this period were the International Criminal Police Organisation (Interpol), which launched its international pursuit of law-breakers, the World Zionist Congress, founded in 1897, and the League of Nations in 1923. The International Red Cross dates back to 1863, and the Save the Children Fund was started in 1919. In addition, the first international initiatives in wildlife conservation were taken around the turn of the 20th century.

The developments outlined here all contributed to the idea that the world was a totality, and to the emergence of a growing global consciousness. This period saw the establishment of important features of a global awareness. Specific events, such as the World Fair of 1851 and the modern Olympic Games, which were first held in 1896, were indicative of this global feeling. It was also facilitated by the development of global travel, which became an option for the wealthy. For example, Thomas Cook led his first round-the-world excursion in 1872.

In summary, during this incipient phase of globalisation, the sense of a society operating across national boundaries appeared in many more forms and with greater intensity than in prior times. However, it is important to recognise that the extent and depth of this globalisation bear no comparison with developments since the 1960s.

The phase of full-scale globalisation, 1950 onwards

In this period, developments in communications, production and markets have led to a growing awareness of the interconnectedness and interdependence of human activities. We see the rise of ideas about the global economy and the global environment, and discussions about a 'global culture'.

One of the most striking features of the latest phase of globalisation has been the development of electronic communications. Direct dialling between countries was introduced in 1963, and satellite and fibre-optic cables have transformed the means of communication. Some indication of the scale of these changes can be seen in the fact that the number of telephone connection points increased from 150 million fixed lines in 1965 to 851 million by 1998. Another example is that of fax machines, which came on the market in the mid-1980s and have expanded to the point at which there are nearly 30 million worldwide.

Perhaps the most potent symbol of the transformation in communications is the Internet. Closely linked is the advent of e-mail, which offers near instantaneous communication via computer.

Case study: The Internet

The Internet, which emerged in the 1980s and has expanded into the 1990s and beyond, is a global network that links individual computers. Together, the Internet, mobile telephones and satellite networks have shrunk space and time. The number of Internet hosts rose from less than 100 000 in 1988 to more than 36 million in 1998. The Internet is the fastest-growing tool of communication ever. While it took 38 years for radio to notch up 50 million users, and television 13 years, the 50 million mark was reached for the Internet in just four years. However, it is easy to overlook the fact that the use of the Internet is highly uneven. If the Internet is the symbol of globalisation, it suggests that the effects of globalisation are unequally distributed. Some examples will serve to highlight this uneven process (**2.2**). In Cambodia in 1996, there was less than one telephone for every 100 people. By contrast, in Monaco there were 99 telephones for every 100 people.

Figure 2.2 The leading Internet users, by nation

	Internet hosts per 1000 of population
Finland	108
USA	88
Norway	71
Canada	53
New Zealand	49
Australia	42
Sweden	35
Netherlands	35
Switzerland	27
UK	23

While there is a tendency to see the Internet as an essentially democratic technology, a number of important features of its use are becoming apparent:

- Internet use is related to income. For example, the average South African user had an income seven times the national average. In the UK, 30 per cent of users had annual salaries above £60 000.
- Internet use is related to education. Globally, 30 per cent of users have at least one university degree. In the UK, the figure is 50 per cent.
- Internet use is related to gender. Women accounted for 38 per cent of users in the USA, 17 per cent in Japan, 7 per cent in China and only 4 per cent in the Arab states.
- Internet use is related to age. The average age of users in the USA is 36, while in China and the UK, it is less than 30.
- English is used in almost 80 per cent of websites, but only one in ten people worldwide speaks English.

Figure 2.3 Internet users – a global enclave

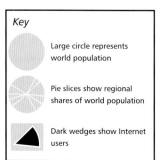

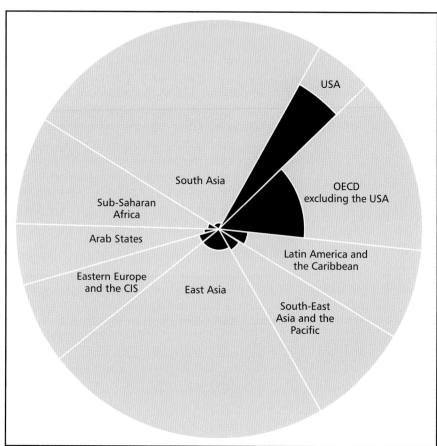

These features suggest that, rather than heralding the dawn of on-line democracy, the present patterns of information and communications technology use are tending to reinforce existing uneven patterns of development (**2.3**).

The sense that we live in 'one world' is heightened by the shared experience of television, which means that the same event can be viewed simultaneously by people all over the world. The first live satellite broadcast was a Beatles concert in 1967. Since then, there has been a range of global events, such as Moon landings, sporting events and even televised wars (such as the Gulf War in the early 1990s). An indication of the burgeoning importance of television is the fact that television density doubled from 121 per 1000 of the world population in 1980 to 235 per 1000 in 1995.

These developments in communications are accompanied by an increasingly complex global economy. A walk around any supermarket will reveal the existence of global goods. Retail distributors have also taken on a global dimension; for example, as in the case of the Italian-owned clothing retailer Benetton, the Japanese-owned 7-Eleven convenience store and the Swedish-based IKEA furniture warehouses. Alternatively, the global consumer, armed with credit cards and television, telephone or Internet, can shop around the world without leaving the house.

The emergence of global markets for goods and services is linked to global production. Increasingly, TNCs have emerged, which have off-loaded aspects of production to low-wage sites, especially in the developing countries. Much of this global production has been linked to the growth of Export Processing Zones in developing countries. These seek to attract foreign investment in which corporations may enjoy subsidies, tax breaks and the suspension of certain aspects of labour legislation.

Alongside these developments in the latest stage of full-scale globalisation is a growing awareness of global ecological issues. Since the 1960s, millions of people worldwide have joined environmental non-governmental organisations (NGOs) such as the World Wide Fund for Nature and Greenpeace. These issues are discussed in more detail in a later chapter. However, it is worth noting three particular issues that have been part of this growing awareness of threats to the global environment.

First, the depletion of stratospheric ozone was recognised from the 1960s and raised alarm in the 1980s. The main culprit was chlorofluorocarbons (CFCs), which were widely used in industrial and consumer products from the 1950s onwards. Second, there is the concern with so-called 'global warming', which is the result of the human-induced increase in the emission of greenhouse gases. This increase started with the beginnings of industrialisation from the middle of the 18th century, but the steep rise in emissions dates from the 1950s. The third issue is the loss of biological diversity. It is estimated that three-quarters of the world's crop varieties were lost in the course of the 20th century. When a species is lost, whole packages of genes disappear.

These environmental concerns are part of a continued growth of global consciousness linked to full-scale globalisation. Increases in global communications, global products, global money flows and organisations have made large proportions of humanity more aware of the world as a single place. For example, some 425 million holidays abroad were taken in 1990. Even when people are unable to move physically, global consciousness is facilitated by television, which – on a daily basis – takes even the armchair viewer across the planet in an instant.

Review

4 Construct a timeline that shows significant dates and events in the process of globalisation.

5 Write a short account of the Internet, based on the information contained in 2.3.

SECTION D

The causes of globalisation

One of the most influential accounts of globalisation is that provided by the economic geographer Peter Dicken (1998), in his book *Global Shift*. He argues that the economically developed countries have all shown marked declines in their percentage share of world manufacturing production since 1948. This has been accompanied by rising industrial production in Japan, and also in the former communist countries. Finally, a number of newly industrialising countries have increased their importance in terms of global manufacturing production.

Figure 2.4 A comparison between some TNC sales and the GNP of selected countries

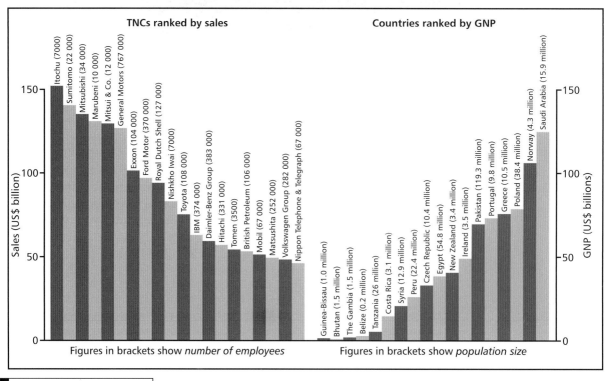

The driving force behind this process of change in the world distribution of production has been the growing influence of the TNCs (**2.4**). In order to increase their profits, such firms have sought out global markets to increase their sales volume. Increased production runs can lead to significant economies of scale and thereby raise profit margins. They have been able to produce goods through developing sources of material and labour at various locations. This allows them to seek out optimal locations and thereby lower their production costs. There are important debates about the effects of these strategies. It has been argued that TNCs have sought to develop global strategies in order to overcome barriers of 'place'. For instance, firms can now seek to locate near to sources of cheap labour, or to avoid countries where social benefits and taxation are high. In addition, they can avoid production in countries whose governments pursue economic policies that are less attractive to business.

Such processes of globalisation could not occur without innovations in transport, communications and data processing. Some writers have suggested that technological change has been the single driving force of globalisation. The speed and capacity of aircraft has increased, especially with the advent of commercial jets in the 1950s and of supersonic carriers in the early 1970s. Optical fibres have acquired ever-rising capacities since their invention in the late 1960s. The maximum load of a single strand of fibre optic cable increased to 6000 simultaneous voice conversations by the early 1980s and to 600 000 concurrent telephone calls by the mid-1990s.

Case study: Come on Barbie, let's go party

Barbie is a doll made from plastic injected into moulds at two factories in south China, adjacent to Hong Kong, one in Indonesia and one in Malaysia. The first Barbie was produced in Japan in 1959. As costs rose in Japan, production was moved to other sites in Asia. The plastic is made from ethylene, refined from Saudi Arabian oil, which is turned into pellets by a firm in Taiwan. Barbie's nylon hair comes from Japan. The cardboard packaging is made in the USA. The manufacturing and packaging are managed from Hong Kong.

Making Barbie is a labour-intensive process. Workers must integrate plastic moulds, sew clothing and paint the details on the dolls. These tasks cannot be performed by machines. The two plants in China employ about 11 000 workers, mainly unmarried women between 18 and 23 from peasant families in poor regions of China, brought to work in the factories for between two and five years.

Of Mattel's 26 000 employees worldwide, only about 6000 work in the USA. In 1981, at the Philippines' Bataan Export Processing Zone, 3000 workers went on strike to protest against a violation of a minimum starting wage agreement. But wages were only part of the issue. It has been suggested that Mattel had offered 'prizes' to female workers who had undergone sterilisation. Workers earn between $4 and $7 a day for 12 hours' work. Apart from low wages, employees suffer respiratory problems, as well as hair and memory loss, muscular pain, vomiting, sleep disorders and irregular menstrual cycles.

Review

6 'Transnational corporations are the driving force of globalisation.' Explain what you understand by this statement.

7 Explain the significance of advances in transport and communication to globalisation.

This chapter has attempted to give something of the flavour of globalisation. It is a process with a long history, but it is the acceleration of the process during the past 25 years or so that makes the greatest impression. The factors driving that acceleration include the emergence of TNCs as powerful key players, the creation of spatially dispersed production chains (such as the one involved in the manufacture of Barbie dolls), plus advances in the technologies of both transport and communications which have drastically shrunk the world.

The impacts of globalisation

One of the most potent images associated with 'global thinking' is the famous view of the Earth from space (**3.1**). Perhaps no other image is so effective in reminding people that we share a common home. Significantly, this image has been taken up by those individuals and organisations who seek to raise our awareness of the environmental costs of development. It is impossible to draw up a balance sheet to assess the impact of globalisation on human society and the environment. However, the following sections discuss just some of the impacts of globalisation. The final part of the chapter examines some of the different views that prevail about the whole process.

Figure 3.1 The Earth from space

SECTION A

Global cities

One of the most striking outcomes of globalisation has been the emergence of a new super-league of cities. The league is made up mainly of cities that have been chosen by the TNCs as the locations for their corporate and regional headquarters. Inevitably, such cities enjoy strategic locations in the global transport and communications networks. Inevitably, too, such cities have become the power bases of globalisation. Peter Dicken has suggested that the league table is a two-tiered structure, with the upper one comprising London, New York and Tokyo, and the lower one made up of the likes of Frankfurt, San Francisco, Buenos Aires and Seoul.

Case study: Seoul, South Korea

Over the past decade, Seoul's connections with the world have expanded and intensified. Global economic forces have led to the opening up of the South Korean economy. Inward investment has grown, most of it in the service sector – in, for example, hotels, stock markets, financial firms and trading companies. Many famous international hotel chains have set up operations in Seoul. A key event was the 1988 Seoul Olympics, which greatly boosted the city's economy, as well as global awareness of it. Perhaps the most visible sign of foreign penetration can be seen in the growing number of fast-food and convenience stores in Seoul.

McDonald's is one of the favourite haunts of schoolchildren. At the same time, South Korean firms have sought to make investments in other countries. Developing countries in Asia, especially China and the countries of South-East Asia, have been favoured locations because of their low wages, cultural similarity, local markets and rich natural resources. The charge has been led by a number of Seoul-based TNCs, including Samsung, Hyundai, Daewoo and LG.

Figure 3.2 Seoul – a global city

The globalisation of Seoul's economy has not been restricted to flows of capital. International movements of people have also increased. While the scale of domestic or rural–urban migration from other parts of South Korea has decreased from a peak in the 1980s, the influx of foreign workers (both legal and illegal) has swollen considerably over the past few years.

Seoul was founded in 1394, but even as recently as the end of the Korean War, in 1953, its population was less than 1 million and South Korea was a predominantly rural country. But since then rural–urban migration has brought about rapid urban growth and industrialisation, and today South Korea is one of the most urbanised countries in the world. Seoul is now home to 11 million people, and throughout its history has had a relatively homogenous character. A single ethnicity, a common language and South Korea's geographical isolation have led to a coherent cultural tradition. However, in the wake of globalisation,

'Koreanness' has been challenged by external influences. Seoulers have begun to consume more goods produced abroad. Foreign workers have been encouraged to come in. The streets of South Korea have been opened up to people from different nations and cultures. Hollywood films are released in Seoul and many American cultural products are readily available. The Seoul Olympics enabled Seoulers to experience and appreciate other cultures. The Olympics drew hundreds of thousands of foreign visitors, and the city now seeks to promote itself as a 'true world city'. In Seoul today, many professional people have been educated abroad, particularly in the USA. Many people learn English. Seoul is increasingly becoming an important site for global tourism.

Thanks to its recent successes, Seoul now suffers from chronic traffic congestion. Exhaust fumes are a problem, because the city sits in a basin and pollution tends to become trapped, leaving a haze over the city that blocks out the sun. Another big problem is waste disposal. Recycling is now much encouraged but, even so, refuse has created a mountain of rubbish that can be seen across the River Han from Seoul's airport. The city's water supply comes primarily from this river, which until recently also received most of the city's untreated sewage.

The financial crisis in the latter part of 1997 shocked the South Korean government and revealed the way in which globalisation has important political implications. The government was accused of financial corruption and inexperience in dealing with global economic trends. The IMF bail-out package strongly requested the South Korean government to follow free-market principles. If this is done, then Seoul's future as a global city looks assured.

Review

1 Find out which other cities can justifiably claim to be 'global cities'. Besides the presence of TNCs, what other features do they have in common?

2 Make a list of the evidence that suggests that Seoul's recent growth can be linked to globalisation.

3 Make a two-column table that lists the costs and benefits of being a global city.

The state of the environment

Critics of globalisation argue that the technologies associated with it tend to be highly polluting. For instance, aircraft are an important source of pollution, as are the motor-powered ships that support global trade. In addition, the energy to power global communications is generated using nuclear and fossil fuels, whose by-products contaminate the environment. While there has been an increase in levels of recycling in recent decades, critics point out that the actual amounts recycled are small in comparison with the greatly increased turnover in consumer goods, which has added to the volume of non-degradable solid wastes.

Figure 3.3 Globalisation carries with it environmental costs

The environmental impacts of globalisation are not distributed equally, since those who are able to afford it can buy themselves environments that are largely free from the worst effects. For example, some companies have sought to locate their operations in countries where environmental regulations are less stringent. In addition, as governments in the economically developed countries have either restricted or banned certain tobacco products, pharmaceuticals and pesticides, global marketing has created new markets for many of these goods in the developing countries. Nearly one-third of the pesticides exported from the developed countries have been outlawed, unregistered or withdrawn in the country of manufacture. There is a burgeoning trade in toxic wastes, as firms seek to dump waste in other countries. According to one commentator, firms made over 500 attempts between 1989 and 1994 to export a total of more than 200 million tonnes of waste from the OECD countries to the developing countries. Apart from these direct examples, it is also suggested that the imperative of increasing the market share, which is central to a global capitalist economy, has led to the destruction of environments. For instance, the drive to intensify exports has led to the over-use of resources, and governments have abandoned environmental projects and policies in an effort to improve short-term economic goals.

In all of this, we have made no mention of some of the potential impacts of environmental change. In response to these global environmental problems, governments have increasingly sought to manage the impact of economic activity on the natural environment. These attempts are linked to the idea of sustainable development, which seeks to promote forms of development that have little long-term impact on the environment (see **Chapter 6**).

Review

4 Debate with your fellow students the proposition that globalisation incurs inevitable environmental costs.

A widening gap

In addition to the environmental impacts, critics have argued that, during the period of intensive globalisation, the general welfare gap between the rich and poor nations has grown. As a general indicator, the aggregate income in 1960 of the countries with the richest fifth of the world's population was 30 times greater than the aggregate income of the countries with the poorest fifth. By 1997, this ratio had grown to 74 : 1. While a few previously 'less-developed' countries have become NICs during this period, most of these countries have experienced little improvement in the general welfare of their populations.

An indication of the uneven distribution of the processes of globalisation can be gained through a consideration of the infrastructure for global communications. The countries with the richest fifth of the world's population have 74 per cent of all telephone lines, while the poorest fifth have just 1.5 per cent. *The Financial Times* has reported that in the mid-1990s there were more telephones in Tokyo than in the whole of Africa. In 1994, the OECD countries accounted for 94 per cent of the market in packaged computer software. In spite of the idea of a global market for global products, most of these products have circulated in the developed world. For instance, consumers in 13 countries have accounted for 80 per cent of the world market in music recordings. In spite of the attractiveness of the idea of a global economy, it is European, Japanese and US currencies that dominate global transactions, not the Brazilian real or the Thai baht. While residents of developed countries have acquired several hundred million global credit cards in order to lubricate their transactions, the 1.2 billion inhabitants of China between them held only 14 million between them.

These figures give some idea of the uneven development of globalisation. However, they do not begin to explain some of the processes that lead to such patterns. It might be thought that the growth of mechanisms of global government should regulate the processes of globalisation. In reality, though, the richer countries have been able to use their economic power to make sure that their interests are secure. For example, the G8 governments currently control more than 45 per cent of the votes on the IMF Executive Board while, collectively, 43 governments in Africa control less than 5 per cent.

So far, we have discussed the impacts of globalisation through a discussion of the general pattern between different countries. As we saw in **Chapter 1**, a major problem of making generalisations about countries is that they tend to gloss over some of the important divisions that exist *within* countries. One major way in which globalisation has widened the gaps in the social class structure relates to access. Although we live in a 'free' economy, access is by no means 'open' to all.

Review

5 Explain why it is that globalisation appears to widen the gap between the rich and the poor countries, and between rich and poor people.

Women in the workforce

Feminist geographers have been interested in the ways in which the processes associated with globalisation affect the lives of women. The process of global shift discussed by Peter Dicken has given women increased opportunities to undertake paid work. Female labour has played a major part in the expanding service economy of global information, global communications, global retailing and global finance. Women have also occupied a large proportion of jobs in global manufacturing. For example, 4 million women held positions in 200 Export Processing Zones (EPZs) in the South (in the sense of the Brandt Report of 1981) alone as of 1994, an increase of 1.3 million over 1986. In many ways, this represents the

feminisation of the labour process. While the quantity of female labour has unquestionably increased, the quality of this labour is more doubtful. Critics have argued that many of the new workplaces are essentially 'electronic sweatshops' – highly stressful and poorly remunerated. There is a strong gender division of labour, with men taking most of the highly salaried positions in management, whereas women have provided most of the low-paid clerical work in the backroom offices.

Jobs in global manufacturing in Export Processing Zones arguably offer women better pay and benefits than other work, and are often highly sought after. However, many of these positions are characterised by highly 'flexible' working conditions. While the jobs that we have been discussing here are all part of the formal sector of the global economy, we should also consider the changes in the informal sectors, where expanded global markets have led to enlarged job 'opportunities' for women. These include a number of highly questionable roles, such as domestic servants, mail-order brides and prostitutes. For example, between 1988 and 1992 some 286 000 Filipinos and 50 000 Thai women arrived in Japan as 'entertainers'.

Review

6 To what extent do you agree with the view that globalisation has created opportunities for women?

SECTION E

People on the move

Figure **3.4** shows some of the major voluntary migration flows. Processes of globalisation are inextricably linked to the mobility of people. Migration is classically seen in terms of push and pull factors. There is no doubt that globalisation has created much employment – albeit in favoured locations – and that modern transport is a facilitator. For millions of people, employment and transport have provided the incentive and the means to move locally, regionally or internationally. In many cases, that incentive has been reinforced by unemployment and poverty.

Contemporary migration stands at new levels – never before in human history have so many people been on the move. It is estimated that 125 million people, or 2 per cent of the world's population, are migrants of some sort. The era of globalisation is directly linked to this rise in the mobility of people. The developed countries, or those parts of the developing world where there are opportunities for work, act as magnets for people who are seeking economic prosperity. In the oil-rich countries of Kuwait and Saudi Arabia, the labour force is largely made up of foreign migrants. Seven industrial countries are the home for one-third of the world's migrants. However, this image of the mobile world, with people on the move, does need to be qualified. For example, it is reckoned that only 2 per cent of the world's population resides outside the country in which they were born, and even in the USA – the world's wealthiest nation – only 9 per cent of the population holds a valid passport.

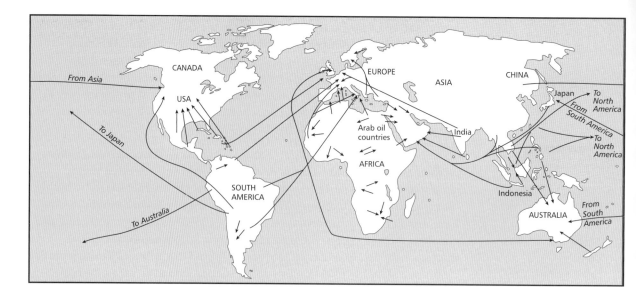

Figure 3.4 Major global migration flows since 1973

While mobility offers opportunities for some, for others it is a curse. For example, some governments are increasingly uneasy about volumes of immigration. More significant is that fact that many people are subject to involuntary migration, as the result of war, persecution, famine and environmental destruction. The UN estimate that, currently, some 27 million (or about one-fifth of the migrant population) are refugees. More than half of these are in Africa or western Asia. It is ironic that in this age of globalisation, and given the trend for us all of us to become members of the global village, the movement of refugees is currently at record levels.

Review

7 Why might governments be uneasy about rising volumes of immigration?

8 Summarise what you see as the costs and benefits of globalisation under the following headings: economic, social, environmental.

Views on globalisation

A most important point raised in this discussion is that globalisation is experienced by different people in different places. Indeed, some experts are sceptical that globalisation represents a significant change in the way in which the world operates. In any case, it is important to recognise that there are important arguments about the nature, extent and desirability of globalisation (**3.5**). It is possible to identify three major viewpoints about globalisation. These are the neo-liberal view, the reformist view and the radical view.

Criterion	Pros	Cons
Environment	Global consciousness has led to greater ecological awareness. Technologies of globalisation have improved means to monitor the environment. There has been a growth of international co-operation in management of the environment.	Many global activities are heavily polluting. Global competition has led to overuse and/or misuse of environments and lowering of environmental standards. Global ecological changes have led to uncertainty and fear about the future.
Poverty and subsistence	Global capitalism has led to rapid welfare rises in the NICs.	Few countries have achieved NIC status. Economic restructuring – as a result of globalisation – has had detrimental effects on developing countries. The debt crisis has seriously hampered efforts to alleviate poverty.
Employment	TNCs and global industries have generated millions of new jobs.	Relocation of TNCs has brought job losses and fears for job security. Global capitalism is generally less labour intensive.
Culture	Global links have increased opportunities for self-development (for example, global travel and interaction). Global technologies have reinvigorated some declining cultures.	Globalisation has been linked to the loss of some traditional cultures. The 'speed-up' of economic and social life has led to greater insecurity and fear of the future.

Figure 3.5 The good and bad of globalisation

Neo-liberal views of globalisation

For neo-liberals, processes of economic and political globalisation are to be welcomed. Neo-liberals argue that globalisation should be accompanied by a large-scale retreat of official regulation and government intervention. They argue that in order to maximise economic efficiency, limitations of movements between countries of money, goods, services and capital – and, more controversially, people – should be minimised. They favour the removal of state controls on prices, wages and exchange rates. In addition, they favour the privatisation of state-controlled industries.

Neo-liberalism is the dominant way of thinking about globalisation. Many governments – including those of the UK and the USA – have adopted neo-liberal policies, especially since the early 1980s. The IMF, the WTO and the OECD have all linked globalisation with the liberalisation of trade. Indeed, in the late 20th century neo-liberal ideas gained widespread acceptance as common sense. For example, it has become increasingly accepted that:

- the market is more efficient than the state in running economic affairs
- free enterprise works
- governments need to minimise their public spending

- private firms should seek to maximise their profits with minimal interference.

Reformist views of globalisation

Reformists are more sceptical of the benefits of globalisation. While they recognise that global capitalism can be a major force for social good, they argue that the achievement of this good requires careful management. Indeed, they argue that, left to its own devices, capitalism tends to produce unacceptable personal, social and environmental costs. To counter these, reformists propose a variety of policies that promote the positive side of capitalism and counter its negative potential. For example, they argue for controls on the international movement of resources when these might lead to serious environmental or social damage. They argue for official guarantees of minimum standards, such as:

- basic incomes
- protection rights and environmental controls
- policies to protect the rights of marginalised groups or minorities.

In response to the development of neo-liberal policies that rejected the idea of governments seeking to steer capitalism, reformists increasingly argue that bodies such as the IMF should devise ways to ensure that there is greater stability and justice in the global economy. Indeed, the late 1990s saw the emergence of challenges to the neo-liberal model of globalisation. Social democratic parties gained political power and sought to argue for a 'third way' between the state and the market. For instance, in 1995 the UN Secretary General argued against globalisation without control, while organisations such as the International Labour Organisation have promoted greater protection rights for workers in global capitalism. The UNDP popularises global reform proposals through its annual *Human Development Report*. A good and readable account of a reformist approach to globalisation can be found in the journalist Will Hutton's book *The State We're In*.

Radical views of globalisation

There are a number of other critiques of global capitalism that are more radical in their analysis. These seek to attack the bases of globalisation. One approach is the traditionalist critique, that seeks to reverse the tide of globalisation. According to this view, globalisation has the effect of destroying established ways of living. Traditionalists call for economic nationalism, the closing of boundaries, religious revivalism and radical environmentalism. Economic nationalism emphasises the need for self-determination in economic policies, even if this involves de-linking from global economic networks. Religious revivalists amongst some Buddhists, Christians, Hindus and Muslims have 'gone local' to retrieve the original beliefs and practices of their faiths. (You might look at B. Barber's book *Jihad vs. McWorld,* which sees the current process of globalisation of the world as a struggle of the West versus the rest.)

Global socialists argue that there is considerable potential for international movements of workers, women and other oppressed groups to organise a post-capitalist world. Others argue that globalisation allows for us to recognise a greater diversity of knowledge and culture. The anti-capitalist protests in Seattle in 1999 and in Prague in 2000 are examples of the activities of those who are sceptical of the social and environmental benefits resulting from globalisation (**3.5**).

In this chapter, we have considered the impacts of, and arguments about, globalisation. An important point to emerge is that the processes of globalisation impact differently on different people in different places, and that the benefits and costs of those processes are unevenly distributed. This leads to the idea that globalisation is not a neutral process, but is unavoidably linked to wider questions about the type of society that we want to live in.

Enquiry

Read the following extract from a newspaper paper article by Andrews Simms, which was published in *The Guardian* on 20 November 1996:

Trading world places
... The world is being brought closer together by information technology and trade, and at the same time as it is being driven further apart by gaps between rich and poor. In the last decade, politics and economics have been shifting like great geological, continental plates. The resulting friction has causes human earthquakes.

For all the goodwill, we are failing to meet the scale of the challenge. Conflict and the breakdown of states are destroying communities and creating millions of refugees. The dynamic is the same North and South. There are refugees in Europe as much as in Africa. The teenager sleeping in the doorway of an expensive London shop and the farmer in Africa who cannot feed and care for her family are suffering the failures of the same economic system.

The creed of free market economists – privatisation and leaving big companies to regulate themselves, maximising profits at all costs – is now influential in all poor countries ... The same system has hold in rich Northern countries too. Unemployment, homelessness and poverty are the result in both places.

The development movement was founded on the idea that poverty was elsewhere, in the Third World. It was an idea that assumed that the First World and its programme of modernisation had all the answers. Looking back it seems a strange idea. Now it is absolutely false.

Individuals and agencies, here and overseas, who have first-hand experience of what it means to be marginalised, must share their knowledge. Shelter, the campaign against homelessness, could speak about the human costs of structural adjustment in Britain ..., while Christian Aid tells of homelessness in Africa and Latin America. It may be that a micro-credit scheme making low interest loans to women heads of poor families in Bangladesh might be as successful on a poverty-stricken estate in Manchester. Such programmes are now working among the poorest communities of America's mega-cities. Poverty groups may now surge ahead with a creative programme that began in Asia. That's global partnership.

At the moment, one side has all the power in a relationship based on giving emergency relief and traditional aid. International trade rules favour the rich against the poor. These are yesterday's rules and we need to change them in the light of global partnerships. Truly imaginative partnerships for long-term development, however, utilise positive and far deeper parts of the human character – wisdom, wit, courage, generosity of spirit and cheerfulness. These are the building blocks of hope.

Discuss the article with other members of your group:

1   What view does the author have? Does he adopt a neo-liberal, reformist or radical view of globalisation? Justify your answer.

2   When you are satisfied that you understand the points the article is making, draft a letter in reply to the author, in which you seek to argue against the position that he has adopted.

States of development

In previous chapters, we have examined the various theories that geographers have put forward to explain development and the idea of globalisation. In this chapter, our attention turns to describing and explaining some of the patterns of development in the contemporary world. In attempting to do this, there are two difficulties. First, as discussed in **Chapter 1**, the question of deciding how to measure development is fraught with difficulty. The problem is essentially about the relative weight given to economic measures of development as opposed to social measures. Second, there is the question of scale. This problem is about the extent to which we can make generalisations about whole regions of the world, such as Europe or Asia, or whether we should focus our attention on particular examples or case studies of specific places. This chapter does not claim to have a definitive answer. However, it does attempt to resolve the problems. In what follows, accounts of three major world regions, and an overview of their patterns of economic and social development, are presented. Within each section, both general patterns and particular examples are discussed. These sections are not supposed to be the last word on this issue. Indeed, it is suggested that, as someone who is studying A-level geography, you should seek to read other accounts of development and build up your own understanding of these issues, using the resources suggested at the end of this book.

SECTION A

Economic and social development in Latin America

General background

Most Latin American economies fit into the broad middle-income category set by the World Bank (**4.1**). Within the Latin American region, the 'Southern Cone' states have the highest GNP per capita, with Argentina having a GNP per capita of over $8000 in 1998. Venezuela and Mexico, the region's leading oil producers, also rank well, although both slipped in the 1990s. The countries with the lowest incomes lie in Central America and the Andes. In 1998, Nicaragua, Honduras and Bolivia all had per capita GNP figures lower than $1000 (**4.2**).

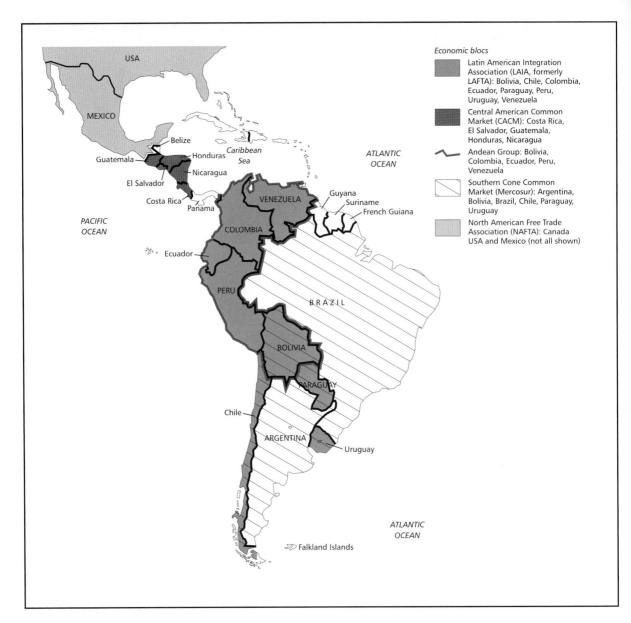

Economic blocs

Latin American Integration Association (LAIA, formerly LAFTA): Bolivia, Chile, Colombia, Ecuador, Paraguay, Peru, Uruguay, Venezuela

Central American Common Market (CACM): Costa Rica, El Salvador, Guatemala, Honduras, Nicaragua

Andean Group: Bolivia, Colombia, Ecuador, Peru, Venezuela

Southern Cone Common Market (Mercosur): Argentina, Bolivia, Brazil, Chile, Paraguay, Uruguay

North American Free Trade Association (NAFTA): Canada USA and Mexico (not all shown)

Figure 4.1 The economic blocs of Latin America

Economic development

From the 1950s onwards, Latin American countries experimented with various development strategies, from closed economies reliant on import substitution to state-run nationalised industries and various attempts at agricultural reform. By the 1960s – the so-called 'Development Decade' – Brazil, Mexico and Argentina all seemed poised to enter the ranks of the industrialised world. The World Bank and the Inter-American Development Bank loaned money for big development projects, such as continental highways, dams, mechanised agriculture and power plants. However, the promised economic development did not materialise. By the

Country	GNP per capita ($US, 1996)	Total GNP (millions of $US, 1996)	Purchasing-power parity ($Intl, 1996)[a]	Real annual growth % per capita (1990–1996)
Costa Rica	2 640	9 081	6 470	2.4
El Salvador	1 700	9 868	2 790	3.5
Guatemala	1 470	16 018	3 820	0.5
Honduras	660	4 012	2 130	1.2
Mexico	3 670	341 718	7 660	−0.3
Nicaragua	380	1 705	1 760	−0.2
Panama	3 080	8 249	7 060	3.6
Argentina	8 380	295 131	9 530	3.9
Bolivia	830	6 302	2 860	1.8
Brazil	4 400	709 591	6 340	2.0
Chile	4 860	70 060	11 700	6.4
Colombia	2 140	80 174	6 720	3.0
Ecuador	1 500	17 531	4 730	0.8
Paraguay	1 850	9 179	3 480	−1.5
Peru	2 420	58 671	4 410	4.8
Uruguay	5 760	18 464	7 760	3.8
Venezuela	3 020	67 333	8 130	−0.3

Figure 4.2 Latin America: economic indicators

[a]The '$Intl' (international dollar) is the standard measure for purchasing-power parity

1980s, much of this momentum had been lost. For instance, Argentina ranked only 34th in the world in 1995, whereas in 1960 its GNP per capita had been higher than that of Japan.

Since the 1960s, most government development policies in Latin American states have emphasised the importance of manufacturing. The result is that at least 15–20 per cent of the labour force in Mexico, Argentina, Peru, Brazil, Chile, Colombia, Uruguay and Venezuela is found in manufacturing. Agricultural production increased with the application of Green Revolution technology and mechanisation. In the process, people were pushed off the land and moved to the large urban centres in search of work. The cities could not provide enough jobs to absorb this influx of migrants, many of whom found their own place in the urban informal economy.

By the 1990s, Latin American governments and the World Bank were promoting neo-liberalism as the model of economic development. Neo-liberal policies stress privatisation, the production of goods for export and the opening of the economy to competition. An often-cited example of the success of neo-liberal policies is that of Chile. Its economic growth rate between 1985 and 1994 averaged 6.2 per cent, better than that of any other country in the region. In 1995 the Chilean economy grew by 10.4 per cent, a rate comparable with the so-called 'Asian Tigers'. However, it may be that Chile's achievements are not transferable to other nations. The moves to privatise state-owned businesses and open the economy were made by an oppressive military dictatorship, under which opposition was not tolerated. However, even in a prosperous city such as Santiago, there are important contrasts in the lives of Chilean people. Many people work in the **informal sector** of the economy, engaged in activities that escape government regulation, registration or taxation.

Social development

The case of Santiago reminds us that any discussion of development must attempt to go beyond the veneer of statistical data and consider other dimensions of the quality of life (**3.3**). On a broad scale, Latin America has

Country	Life expectancy at birth (years)		Under age 5 mortality (per 1000 live births)		Secondary school enrolment (%)		Female labour force participation (% of total)
	Male	Female	Male	Female	Male	Female	
Costa Rica	73	78	112	16	45	49	30
El Salvador	65	72	210	40	27	30	35
Guatemala	63	68	205	67	25	23	27
Honduras	66	71	203	38	29	37	30
Mexico	69	75	141	32	57	58	31
Nicaragua	63	68	209	60	39	44	36
Panama	71	77	104	20	60	65	34
Argentina	69	76	68	27	70	75	31
Bolivia	57	63	252	105	40	34	37
Brazil	64	71	181	60	–	–	35
Chile	72	78	138	15	65	70	32
Colombia	65	73	132	36	57	68	38
Ecuador	66	71	180	40	54	56	27
Paraguay	66	71	90	34	36	38	29
Peru	67	71	236	55	66	60	29
Uruguay	72	78	47	21	–	–	41
Venezuela	70	75	70	24	29	41	33

Figure 4.3 Latin America: social indicators

seen marked improvements in life expectancy, child survival and educational attainment since 1960. Much of this is linked to the activities of grass-roots and non-governmental organisations, which have provided many of the services that state and local governments have been unable or unwilling to provide. Church groups work with people in rural areas to improve water supplies, sanitation and education. Secular groups lobby local government authorities to build schools or to recognise squatters' claims to land.

Aggregate data about the levels of social development tend to obscure wide variations on a number of dimensions; for instance:

- between rural and urban areas
- between regions
- between men and women.

Latin American societies have traditionally been demarcated along lines of gender, based on the cultural traits of *machismo* ascribed to men and *marianismo* ascribed to women. **Machismo** refers to honour, risk-taking and self-confidence, which leads men to demand authority in public and in the home. The female counterpart, **marianismo**, refers to Mary, the mother of Jesus Christ. Women who follow *marianismo* strive to be patient, loving, gentle and willing to suffer in silence. At the same time, women are respected for their higher moral authority. These cultural norms of *machismo* and *marianismo* are breaking down under the pressures of economic and social change. Many Latina women work outside the home, with levels of female participation in the workforce rivalling that found in many European countries.

What effect is globalisation having on the region?

The integration of Latin America into the global economy has a long history. The region was the first to be fully colonised by European countries. Latin American trade has well-established links with Europe and North America. At the present time, there are two important transition zones in the region. The first is along the US–Mexico border. As Mexico becomes more intricately involved with to the US economy, there are likely to be important changes in the linkages between these two countries. Many people see the cultural divide between these two nations as too great but, along the border, these 'distant neighbours' are creating a distinctive cultural zone, with strong influences from each side. The second zone is the Southern Cone. Here the economic and social indicators are so much better than in the Andean countries, and it is possible that these Mercosur countries will increase their influence in the region, and even globally (**4.1**).

Review

1 Study **4.2** and **4.3**.

   a Comment on the diversity of the development patterns found in Latin America.

   b Suggest reasons for the differences in the economic and social indicators.

2 Explain the significance of *machismo* and *marianismo* in the context of development.

SECTION B

The Mexican experience

Mexico provides a useful example of some of the development issues facing countries in Latin America. From the 1940s onwards, the Mexican government actively promoted industrialisation as a means of economic development. This was achieved through supporting the private sector. The goal was industrialisation of the **import substitution** kind, designed to reduce the level of imports and promote self-sufficiency. This involved the manufacture of products that were previously imported from the USA or other economically developed countries. Industrialisation was intended to create employment and improve living standards.

The Mexican government supported industrialisation by subsidising the private sector. It provided rail transport and energy at low prices, and loans at low interest rates. It also set up state-owned firms in certain activities, such as railways, electricity, oil and steel, which were crucial to national economic development. Policies were put in place to protect industries from foreign competition.

The results of these interventions were seemingly impressive. From 1940 to 1970, GDP rose consistently at an annual rate of between 6 and 7 per cent. Even taking into account population growth, GDP per capita increased at around 3.5 per cent annually. However, in the 1970s the Mexican economy faltered, mainly as a result of the private sector's lack of confidence in the government of the time. These problems were postponed following the discovery of major oil reserves and the injection of foreign credit, with the result that by the end of the 1970s economic growth was reaching between 8 and 9 per cent.

Development has had dramatic impacts on Mexican society. Through rural–urban migration, the country has changed from a predominantly rural society to a predominantly urban one. By the 1980s, Mexico City had become the world's most populated city. Mexico's literacy rate rose from 52 per cent in 1940 to 96 per cent in 1990. However, there were drawbacks. The benefits of economic growth were unevenly distributed, and the model of economic development that had been followed led to economic inefficiencies. This contributed to Mexico's debt crisis in the 1980s. In addition, high levels of poverty and income inequality led to periodic political unrest, as students, workers, peasants and the urban poor protested against economic injustice.

Some commentators have suggested that as nations pass through the early stages of modernisation and economic development, income inequality tends to worsen. This is apparently true of Mexico. When the country began its drive to industrialise in the 1940s, government policies designed to improve income distribution were effectively abandoned. A number of factors were important:

■ In the countryside, government policy favoured larger, commercial farmers, who were more productive and better equipped to produce agricultural surpluses for the domestic market and for export. As a result, landlessness increased and many peasants who were unable to compete lost their farms.

■ Although the working class and city poor benefited from the urban bias of many government policies, they were also disadvantaged by restraints on wages, and by poor social services and a lack of employment.

By the 1960s, Mexico's income distribution was amongst the most unequal in the developing world. The gap between the rich and poor widened, as Mexico's economic miracle left behind substantial proportions of the population. In 1980, more than three-quarters of the population still lived in overcrowded housing (**4.4**).

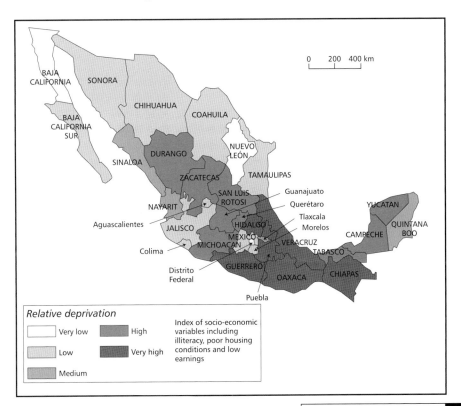

Figure 4.4 Relative deprivation in Mexico, 1980

The economic crisis of the 1980s caused a rethink of the development model. The result was that Mexico's leaders reduced the role of state intervention and opened up the economy to world trade and competition. This has meant a shift to export-oriented growth. In 1986, Mexico joined GATT, the world's most influential trading group (now the WTO), and seven years later it helped to create NAFTA, linking its economy to those of the USA and Canada (**4.1**). Stripped of protection, Mexican firms have been forced to become more competitive in the international market. These moves have been important in reassuring investors that Mexico is committed to involvement in the world market, thus ensuring a business-friendly environment. The government followed a path committed to attracting foreign investment, reducing wages and social spending, and thus keeping inflation low. These reforms imposed enormous costs on the population, especially the poor. Wage increases failed to match the rate of inflation. From 1980 to 1989, per capita GDP declined by 9 per cent. In order to make a living in these conditions, the importance of peasant subsistence farming has increased and a large section of the urban poor are involved in the informal sector, working as street vendors, repair workers and so on.

The political and social costs of the policy of neo-liberalism followed by the Mexican government included the ending of the 71-year rule of the Institutional Revolutionary Party (PRI) in the 2000 elections. The National Action Party (PAN) now form the government of the country. The new president, Vicente Fox, is seeking to develop a Mexican 'Third Way'. This will try to combine those neo-liberal policies that seek to make Mexico part of the global economy (deregulation, competition, tight controls on public spending) with a social agenda that includes pledges to double education spending, increase subsidies for farmers and build health clinics.

The success of this policy depends on the economy being able to deliver high rates of economic growth while keeping inflation low. In signalling his commitment to the NAFTA arrangement, President Fox is hoping to deepen the relationship with the USA and maintain the confidence of foreign investors. This explains his plans to deregulate industries such as oil, electricity and petrochemicals. The result of the integration with the USA and Canada is vividly illustrated by the Mexican assembly plants that line the border with the USA. In the mid-1990s there were more than 2000 of these *maquiladora* plants, employing more than half a million workers, and involved in the assembly of electrical goods, automobiles and clothing. These plants developed from the mid-1960s, when the Mexican government allowed the duty-free import of machinery and components from the USA to be used for manufacturing goods to be exported back to the USA. This process took off in the 1980s, as foreign companies realised profits from the relatively low cost of Mexican labour. For example, a car worker in a General Motors plant in Mexico earns an average of $10 a day, while his American counterpart earns more than $200 a day in wages and benefits.

3 Explain what you understand by the following terms:

- import substitution
- relative deprivation
- *maquiladora*
- neo-liberalism.

4 Give examples of how globalisation is affecting Latin America.

SECTION C

Economic and social development in Sub-Saharan Africa

General background

By most indicators, Sub-Saharan Africa tends to be the poorest and least-developed world region (**4.5**). Only a few African countries, such as Gabon, South Africa, Seychelles and Mauritius, are counted among the middle-income countries of the world. What makes this worse is that the region's economic base actually declined in the 1980s and 1990s. This falling economic output was accompanied by continued population growth over the same period. However, we need to take care to avoid painting a picture of doom and gloom, and consider things in more detail.

Country	GNP per capita ($US, 1996)	Total GNP (millions of $US, 1996)	Purchasing-power parity ($Intl, 1996)	Real annual growth % per capita (1990–1996)
Angola	270	2 972	1 030	–5.6
Benin	350	1 998	1 230	1.9
Botswana	3 020[a]	4 381[a]	7 390	1.3
Burkina Faso	230	2 410	950	–0.1
Burundi	170	1 066	590	–6.4
Cameroon	610	8 356	1 760	–3.8
Cape Verde	1 010	393	2 640	–16.7
Central African Republic	310	1 024	1 430	–1.7
Chad	160	1 035	880	–1.7
Comoros	450	228	1 770	–1.8
Congo	670	1 813	1 410	–4.3
Democratic Republic of Congo	130	5 727	790	–10.4
Djibouti	–	–	–	–
Equatorial Guinea	530	217	2 690	15.9

Country	GNP per capita ($US, 1996)	Total GNP (millions of $US, 1996)	Purchasing-power parity ($Intl, 1996)	Real annual growth % per capita (1990–1996)
Eritrea	–	–	–	–
Ethiopia	100	6 042	500	2.0
Gabon	3 950	4 444	6 300	–1.2
Gambia	–	–	1 280	–0.5
Ghana	360	6 223	1 790	1.5
Guinea	560	3 804	1 720	1.9
Guinea-Bissau	250	270	1 030	0.5
Ivory Coast	660	9 434	1 580	0.2
Kenya	320	8 661	1 130	–0.5
Lesotho	660	1 331	2 380	0.9
Liberia	–	–	–	–
Madagascar	250	3 428	900	–2.0
Malawi	180	1 832	690	–0.2
Mali	240	2 422	710	–0.2
Mauritania	470	1 089	1 810	1.7
Mauritius	3 710	4 205	9 000	3.6
Mozambique	80	1 472	500	2.6
Namibia	2 250	3 569	5 390	1.6
Niger	200	1 879	920	–2.3
Nigeria	240	27 599	870	1.2
Réunion	–	–	–	–
Rwanda	190	1 268	630	–8.2
Sao Tomé and Principe	330	45	–	–1.7
Senegal	570	4 856	1 650	–0.6
Seychelles	6 850	526	–	1.5
Sierra Leone	200	925	510	–3.9
Somalia	–	–	–	–
South Africa	3 520	132 455	7 450	–0.2
Sudan	–	–	–	–
Swaziland	1 210	1 122	3 320	–1.2
Tanzania	170	5 174	–	–0.2
Togo	300	1 278	1 650	–3.9
Uganda	300	5 826	1 030	4.0
Zambia	360	3 363	860	–4.8
Zimbabwe	610	6 815	2 220	–1.1

Figure 4.5 Sub-Saharan Africa: economic indicators

[a]Botswana's GNP per capita and total GNP are based on 1995 figures

Economic development

Sub-Saharan Africa is a good example of the need to avoid making hasty generalisations about whole swathes of the Earth's surface for, like most regions, it is marked by significant variations in levels of economic and social development. A number of features are worth noting:

- South Africa (see **Section D**) is the most important economic power in the region. It has a well developed and balanced manufacturing sector, a prosperous agricultural sector and is one of the world's mining superpowers. South Africa is the world's leading gold producer and is a leader in many other minerals as well. However, while South Africa is a wealthy country by African standards, it is also a country divided by marked inequality and severe poverty. The white minority still enjoys a high standard of living denied to the majority of the population.
- A second group of relatively well-off Sub-Saharan countries benefits from substantial oil and mineral reserves. The prime example is Gabon, a country of considerable oil wealth with a population of just 1.2 million. In the south, Namibia and Botswana are examples of countries with small populations and abundant mineral resources, especially diamonds. These countries experienced significant economic growth in the 1990s.
- The Economic Community of West African States is a group of states that have joined together to develop mutual economic interests. The largest of these countries is Nigeria, which has the largest oil reserves in the region. Nigeria has a burgeoning population, and its per capita income is low. In addition, it is a society marked by extremes of wealth and poverty. The majority of Nigerians have seen little of the oil revenues.
- The poorest parts of Sub-Saharan Africa include the Sahel, the Horn and the south-east. In the Sahel, countries such as Mali, Burkina Faso, Niger and Chad have all suffered from long periods of drought and environmental degradation.

Social development

Figure **4.6** shows that Sub-Saharan Africa's figures on life expectancy are among the lowest in the world. Low life expectancy is related to extreme poverty, environmental hazards such as drought, and various environmental and infectious diseases. The apparently successful combating of malaria has suffered a setback in recent years, as the organisms responsible for the disease have developed a resistance to drugs, and the mosquitoes that carry the disease have become resistant to insecticide.

Country	Life expectancy at birth (years)		Under age 5 mortality (per 1000 live births)		Secondary school enrolment (%)		Female labour force participation (% of total)
	Male	Female	Male	Female	Male	Female	
Angola	45	48	345	292	–	–	46
Benin	51	56	310	144	17	7	48
Botswana	40	42	170	56	49	55	46
Burkina Faso	46	47	318	175	11	6	47
Burundi	44	47	255	178	8	5	49
Cameroon	53	56	264	113	32	23	38
Cape Verde	66	73	–	–	21	20	38
Central African Republic	44	48	294	177	17	6	47
Chad	45	50	325	206	13	2	44
Comoros	57	62	–	–	21	17	42
Congo	45	49	220	19	–	–	43
Democratic Republic of Congo	47	51	286	187	33	15	44
Djibouti	47	50	–	–	14	10	40
Equatorial Guinea	46	50	316	–	–	–	35
Eritrea	52	57	–	204	17	13	47
Ethiopia	41	42	294	202	12	11	41
Gabon	52	55	287	154	–	–	44
Gambia	43	47	375	–	25	13	45
Ghana	54	58	215	170	44	28	51
Guinea	43	47	337	226	17	6	47
Guinea-Bissau	41	44	336	235	9	4	40
Ivory Coast	51	54	300	120	33	17	33
Kenya	48	49	202	90	28	23	46
Lesotho	54	55	204	156	22	31	37
Liberia	56	61	288	217	–	–	39
Madagascar	51	53	364	164	14	14	45
Malawi	36	36	365	223	6	3	49
Mali	45	47	400	217	12	6	46
Mauritania	50	53	321	202	19	11	44
Mauritius	67	74	84	23	58	60	32
Mozambique	43	46	331	282	9	6	48
Namibia	42	42	206	79	49	61	41
Niger	45	48	320	320	9	4	44

Country	Life expectancy at birth (years)		Under age 5 mortality (per 1000 live births)		Secondary school enrolment (%)		Female labour force participation (% of total)
	Male	Female	Male	Female	Male	Female	
Nigeria	49	52	204	191	32	27	36
Réunion	75	75	–	–	–	–	42
Rwanda	43	44	191	141	11	9	49
Sao Tomé and Principe	62	65	–	–	–	–	35
Senegal	48	50	303	120	21	11	43
Seychelles	65	76	–	–	–	–	–
Sierra Leone	33	36	384	284	22	12	36
Somalia	45	49	294	211	9	5	43
South Africa	55	60	126	69	71	84	37
Sudan	50	52	292	128	24	19	26
Swaziland	38	41	233	–	51	50	37
Tanzania	45	49	249	167	6	5	49
Togo	56	60	264	135	34	12	40
Uganda	40	41	218	185	14	8	48
Zambia	37	38	220	203	25	14	45
Zimbabwe	40	40	181	83	51	40	44

Figure 4.6 Sub-Saharan Africa: social indicators

It is increasingly recognised that economic and social development in Sub-Saharan Africa depends upon the inclusion and recognition of the role of women. In agriculture, women account for 75 per cent of the labour force that produces more than half of the food consumed in the region. This largely involves subsistence farming, mixed with other forms of domestic work and the sale of any surplus food in local markets. Some research suggests that, in certain states, these informal activities can account for 30–50 per cent of the gross domestic product.

What effect is globalisation having on the region?

Sub-Saharan Africa provides an important lesson in thinking about globalisation, because when we think about places becoming increasingly interconnected, and about ever increasing numbers of goods, services and people moving across the globe, Sub-Saharan Africa tends to be excluded. In terms of trade, Sub-Saharan Africa's connection with the global economy is limited. The level of overall trade is low, both within the region (intraregional) and outside it. Most exports are bound for the EU, especially the former colonial powers. Much of Sub-Saharan Africa lacks the infrastructure to develop more intraregional trade. Only southern Africa has a telecommunications network of any note.

Despite the relatively low levels of trade, Sub-Saharan Africa is linked to the world economy through the flow of financial aid and loans. Some African states, such as Mali, Gabon, Mozambique and Namibia, received more than US$50 per capita in assistance in 1996. This is in marked contrast with flows of private investment, although there are notable exceptions, such as South Africa, Ivory Coast, Ghana and Angola.

According to many commentators, Sub-Saharan Africa is set to experience a political and economic meltdown in the next few decades. Large numbers of unemployed and disaffected young people threaten political instability. Ethnic conflict and the spread of HIV and AIDS add to the region's many problems. Desertification, and other forms of environmental degradation linked to high levels of population growth, threaten the livelihoods of millions of people, as well as the economic foundations of the entire region. Pessimists see the case of Rwanda – a densely populated country torn apart by an ethnic conflict of genocidal proportions – as a portent of things to come. More optimistically, most of Sub-Saharan Africa is sparsely populated and large areas of land could be productively farmed. There are signs of hope in the fact that fertility levels appear to be declining, and there are improvements in health and education (**4.6**).

Review

5 Study **4.5** and **4.6**.
  a Comment on the diversity of the development patterns found in Sub-Saharan Africa.

  b Suggest reasons for the differences in the economic and social indicators.

6 Summarise the optimistic and pessimistic views of the future of Sub-Saharan Africa. Which do you think is the more plausible? Justify your viewpoint.

The South African experience

The current economic situation in the Republic of South Africa cannot be explained without reference to the history of racial segregation and apartheid. The history of modern South Africa dates back to the establishment of a supply station by the Dutch East India Company in Cape Town, in 1652. The Dutch settlers sought to segregate themselves from the aboriginal peoples. The early settlers included French Huguenots and Germans, as well as Dutch burghers, who were mostly farmers. Over time, as white settlers moved into the dry lands to the east of Cape Town, they pushed into areas already occupied by native peoples. In the struggle for land, the native peoples were decimated by war, and by diseases contracted from the white settlers. During the conflicts between the Boers and the native peoples, a distinctive Afrikaner (South African Dutch) identity was developed. As the native peoples were pushed from the land around Cape Town, some survived by migrating northwards and others were incorporated as servants into the growing Boer economy.

By 1806, Britain had established political control over the Cape. Like the Dutch, the British set about acquiring land and setting up boundaries between the European immigrant settlements and the largely Bantu-speaking Nguni and Sotho people. Conflict between native and white peoples was common. Whites claimed increasing control over land and water, as native peoples resisted and then retreated south and westwards.

The mid-19th century saw a series of Kaffir Wars, which were about the control of labour supplies. Missionaries and traders were important in convincing the defeated black people to work as wage labour on white-owned farms or in the white urban areas. The previous Boer policy of strict racial segregation between blacks and Afrikaners was opposed by the British policy of racial mixing, under which blacks were intentionally exposed to white value systems and institutions.

As British influence undermined Dutch control of native peoples, Boer farmers – in the Great Trek of 1836 – moved northwards to areas beyond British influence. The Voortrekers did this in order to preserve their own value system and to protest against the abolition of slavery. They displaced the Sotho and Zulu peoples, and founded republics in Natal, the Orange Free State and the Transvaal. In these areas, the Boers established native reserves and took land from the independent Zulu peoples. The native peoples, whose land was lost, were forced to take part in a cash economy in order to obtain money and to purchase particular types of clothes, which they were required to wear when working or travelling in white urban areas.

The discovery of diamonds near Kimberley in 1887 had the effect of linking white South Africa to the global economy. The discovery led to the establishment of mines, as well as to the construction of the railway network to connect the mines to the ports. Skilled labour, machinery, technology and capital linked South Africa to the world economy. The struggle between the British and the Dutch colonisers to control this trade led eventually to the Anglo-Boer War of 1899–1902.

The mining industry led to the rapid growth of population in the mining centres and in the ports. By 1911, the major diamond- and gold-mining centres (Kimberly, Pretoria–Witwatersrand and Johannesburg) comprised 37 per cent of the total population, with the four ports (Cape Town, Durban, Port Elizabeth and East London) accounting for another 23 per cent. This population increase was the result of increased European migration to South Africa, as well as the temporary migration of black males from their homelands to the mines and urban centres in search of work.

The first half of the 20th century witnessed the strengthening and extension of the Boer principles of racial segregation through territorial segregation. The policy designed to encourage racial segregation was called **apartheid**. Under apartheid, the various peoples of South Africa were divided into formal categories. Black ownership of land was restricted, as was Black settlement. The permanent residence of Blacks in White urban areas was prohibited. The Natives (Urban Areas) Act 1923 defined Blacks as temporary urban residents who were to be repatriated (sent back) to the tribal reserves if not employed. It also made clear that, while in urban areas, Blacks were to be physically, socially and economically separated from the White population (**4.7**).

Figure 4.7 Apartheid involved the segregation of racial groups in all aspects of daily life

The late 1980s saw the beginning of the end of apartheid in South Africa. Nelson Mandela was freed from jail, and President P. W. Botha agreed to the sharing of political power between 'Blacks' and 'Whites'. The Reconstruction and Development Programme was adopted as official government policy in 1994. The first priority was to meet basic needs for jobs, land, housing, clean water, electricity, telecommunications, a clean and healthy environment, nutrition, health care and social welfare.

There have been some important achievements since the end of apartheid, including the connection of 1.3 million homes to electricity and 1 million to water, a feeding scheme in 12 300 primary schools to combat malnutrition, and almost 300 new health clinics in rural areas. However, meeting the objectives of the Reconstruction and Development Programme has required economic growth rates in excess of the population increase of 2 per cent per annum. In the absence of such economic growth, the redistribution of wealth from the richer white sections of the population has become a necessity. In the area of providing low-cost housing, the government was reluctant to intervene in the housing market, which meant that the programme failed to meet its objectives. In the face of mounting dissatisfaction with the failure of the government to deliver, a new economic policy, known as Growth, Employment and Redistribution (GEAR), was put in place. These policies favoured reduced state spending, investment incentives for foreign-owned TNCs, wage restraint, labour-market flexibility and privatisation. The idea was that getting a job was the best way out of poverty, and GEAR promised rapid economic growth, to create 1.35 million jobs by 2000.

However, the employment projections were soon seen to be over-optimistic. In addition, in view of the failure to provide social benefits such as housing, health and education, the neo-liberal policies of the government were criticised. Those policies were having the largest adverse impact on South Africa's poor, largely black majority.

Review

7 In what ways and to what extent does tension between 'Black' and 'White' peoples continue to handicap South Africa's development?

8 Assess the extent to which the processes of globalisation are affecting the development of the Sub-Saharan region.

Economic and social development in South-East Asia

Until recently, economic development in South-East Asia was held up to the world as a model for the new globalised capitalism. The spark for this was investment from Japan, and then from elsewhere, which allowed countries such as Thailand, Malaysia and Indonesia to join the ranks of the 'Tiger' economies, characterised by high annual growth rates (**4.8**). However, since late 1997 the economy of the region has been in a state of crisis. In that time, the currencies of both Thailand and Indonesia have devalued by almost 50 per cent, and other countries have suffered similarly.

As in the case of Sub-Saharan Africa, South-East Asia is a region of very uneven economic and social development. Singapore and Malaysia have been the region's greatest developmental successes, with Singapore transforming itself into one of the world's most prosperous and modern states, and Malaysia attaining the status of one of the world's 'middle-income countries'. In contrast, the three countries of former French Indochina have experienced relatively little economic expansion. This area was the scene of almost continual warfare between 1941 and 1975, and fighting continued in Cambodia until the late 1990s. The example of Vietnam highlights some of the continuing difficulties. The country was reunified in 1975. However, the much hoped for economic growth did not materialise, and things were made worse in the early 1990s by the economic and political collapse of the Soviet Union, Vietnam's main supporter and trading partner. Faced with a trade embargo by the USA, the Vietnamese government began to embrace the free market, seeking to expand its trading partners while retaining a strong communist state. The

Country	GNP per capita ($US, 1996)	Total GNP (millions of $US, 1996)	Puchasing-power parity ($Intl, 1996)	Real annual growth % per capita (1990–1996)
Burma (Myanmar)	–	–	–	3.9
Brunei	–	–	–	–1.5
Cambodia	300	3 088	–	2.9
Indonesia	1 080	213 384	3 310	5.9
Laos	400	1 895	1 250	3.9
Malaysia	4 370	89 800	10 390	6.1
Philippines	1 160	83 289	3 550	1.0
Singapore	30 550	92 987	26 910	6.6
Thailand	2 960	177 476	6 700	6.7
Vietnam	290	21 915	1 570	6.2

Figure 4.8 South-East Asia: economic indicators

result is that Vietnam now welcomes TNCs such as Nike, which are attracted by its relatively low wages and well-educated workforce (**4.9**). The hope is that the free market will unleash the entrepreneurial potential of the Vietnamese people, leading to a new period of economic growth.

The reforms have had some effect, particularly in the formerly capitalist south. However, the TNCs have been slow to invest. Many American TNCs fear that the country's political climate is still too unstable, but TNCs based in South Korea have been more eager to build factories. Some commentators suggest that non-competitive, state-owned industries remain a burden on the Vietnamese economy.

What effect is globalisation having on the region?

In many ways, South-East Asia is typical of the image of the global economy. The Tiger economies have staked their future on integration into the global economy and opened their doors to multinational corporations. Even countries that prided themselves on isolation, such as Vietnam and Myanmar (Burma), are opening their doors to the global economy. The pattern has been uneven, with Singapore, Malaysia and Thailand experiencing the most rapid development. There are costs associated with integration into the global capitalist economy, notably environmental degradation and the harsh discipline of low-wage manufacturing that forms much of the basis for economic development. The 1997 crisis came as a shock to the economies of South-East Asia, and many critics of

Country	Life expectancy at birth (years)		Under age 5 mortality (per 1000 live births)		Secondary school enrolment (%)		Female labour force participation (% of total)
	Male	Female	1960	1995	Male	Female	
Burma (Myanmar)	60	62	237	111	23	23	43
Brunei	70	73	–	–	67	74	34
Cambodia	50	53	217	181	–	–	53
Indonesia	60	64	216	111	48	39	40
Laos	52	55	233	141	31	19	47
Malaysia	70	75	105	17	56	61	37
Philippines	63	69	102	59	71	75	37
Singapore	74	80	40	6	69	71	38
Thailand	67	72	146	33	38	37	46
Vietnam	65	69	219	48	–	–	49

Figure 4.9 South-East Asia: social indicators

globalisation point to the dangers associated with following a path of integration. In addition, there is increasing concern amongst consumers in the developed countries about the conditions under which trainers and clothes produced in South-East Asia are produced, and there is fear of a global boycott.

Another question about the nature of development in South-East Asia relates to the environment. Much development has been dependent on the export of resources such as forest logs, with the result that the region has lost much of its tropical rainforest cover (**4.10**). There is continued pressure by commercial interests to develop this trade further, although this is set against a backdrop of measures that are calling for restraint. Many of the large and growing cities of South-East Asia also face major problems of pollution and traffic congestion.

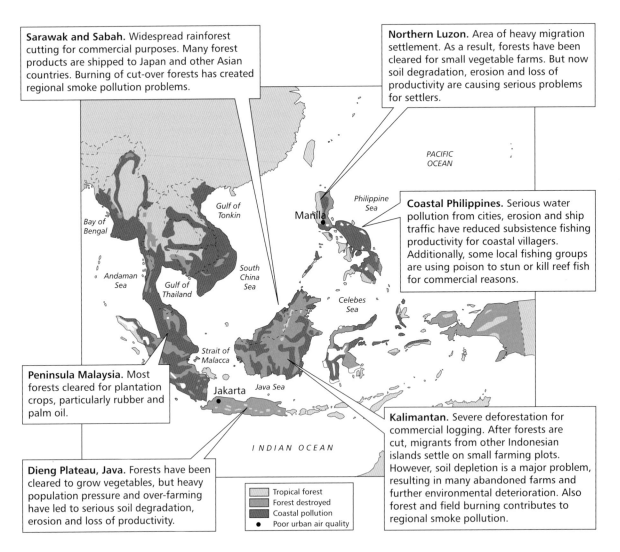

Sarawak and Sabah. Widespread rainforest cutting for commercial purposes. Many forest products are shipped to Japan and other Asian countries. Burning of cut-over forests has created regional smoke pollution problems.

Northern Luzon. Area of heavy migration settlement. As a result, forests have been cleared for small vegetable farms. But now soil degradation, erosion and loss of productivity are causing serious problems for settlers.

Coastal Philippines. Serious water pollution from cities, erosion and ship traffic have reduced subsistence fishing productivity for coastal villagers. Additionally, some local fishing groups are using poison to stun or kill reef fish for commercial reasons.

Peninsula Malaysia. Most forests cleared for plantation crops, particularly rubber and palm oil.

Kalimantan. Severe deforestation for commercial logging. After forests are cut, migrants from other Indonesian islands settle on small farming plots. However, soil depletion is a major problem, resulting in many abandoned farms and further environmental deterioration. Also forest and field burning contributes to regional smoke pollution.

Dieng Plateau, Java. Forests have been cleared to grow vegetables, but heavy population pressure and over-farming have led to serious soil degradation, erosion and loss of productivity.

Tropical forest
Forest destroyed
Coastal pollution
● Poor urban air quality

Figure 4.10 Environmental issues in South-East Asia

SECTION F

The Indonesian experience

Indonesia was once a Dutch colony. The Dutch used the colony as an extraction zone, taking from it tropical crops and other resources. They invested little in infrastructure or education. The population of Java (the main island) increased rapidly in the late 19th and early 20th centuries, and there were serious land shortages. The colonial legacy meant that when Indonesia gained independence in 1949, its economic development was hindered by political instability. However, the economy did begin to expand in the 1970s. This early growth was fuelled by oil exports and the logging of tropical forests. Since then, Indonesia has proved attractive to TNCs, who seized the opportunity to export goods produced by a low-wage workforce. Large Indonesian firms, largely owned by local Chinese families, have also taken advantage of the cheap labour and abundant resources. The government has encouraged technological industries and the economy is now expanding into areas such as car and aeroplane manufacturing.

However, despite economic growth, there are problems. Indonesia's expansion has been dependent on an unsustainable exploitation of natural resources. The country was hit badly by the financial crisis of 1997. In 1998, industrial production declined by 15 per cent, and millions of Indonesians found themselves unable to afford to buy rice, the staple foodstuff. There was also heightened tension between the Chinese community and the rest of the Indonesian population.

There are marked geographical disparities in economic and social development within Indonesia. North-west Java, close to the capital city Jakarta, has boomed; much of the moderately populated and resource-rich of island Sumatra has maintained economic prosperity. However, in the overcrowded rural districts of east and central Java, many peasants have no land or possess only tiny plots, and struggle to make a living. The eastern parts of Indonesia have experienced little economic and social development, and in the outer islands tribal people have suffered as their lands have been lost to outsiders. An example of the types of problem is the tension over Irian Java (or Western New Guinea). After a referendum that

Figure 4.11 A burning forest in Indonesia – some people have argued that the price paid for economic development is an over-exploitation of environmental resources, an issue that is discussed in more detail in **Chapter 5**

many believe was fixed by the Indonesian government, this region joined Indonesia in 1962. The Indonesian government encouraged migration from the overcrowded island of Java. Faced with the loss of their land and the degradation of the environment, the indigenous inhabitants rebelled.

Review

11 To what extent have the benefits of economic globalisation in Indonesia been cancelled out by social and environmental costs?

This chapter has provided a discussion of some of the patterns of economic and social development in different regions of the world. It has highlighted the great diversity that exists in terms of economic and social development, and it has shown how globalisation affects different countries in different ways.

12 For each of the regions discussed in this chapter, show how their patterns of development are being shaped by the processes of globalisation.

13 To what extent do you think the theories of development discussed in **Chapter 1** help to explain the current development patterns of the three regions discussed in this chapter?

14 In the light of what you have read about each of the three regions, which of the paths of globalisation – neo-liberal, reformist or radical – do you think would most suit the development needs of the people? Give your reasons.

Enquiry

Study **4.12**, which gives selected data for a sample of eight countries.

	Land area (km²)	Average annual population growth rate (1990–1997) (%)	GNP per capita ($US, 1997)	Real annual growth % per capita (1990–1996)	Life expectancy at birth (years)		Age under 5 mortality (per 1000 live births)		Secondary school enrolment (%)		Female labour force participation (% of total)
					Male	Female	1963	1993	Male	Female	
Brazil	8 457	1.4	4 720	2	64	71	181	60	–	–	35
Ecuador	277	2.2	1 590	0.8	66	71	180	40	54	56	27
Egypt	995	2	1 180	2.2	65	69	258	59	81	69	29
India	2 973	1.8	390	3.8	59	59	236	122	59	38	32
Indonesia	1 812	1.7	1 110	5.9	60	64	216	111	48	39	40
Niger	1 267	3.3	200	-2.3	45	48	320	320	9	4	44
Poland	304	0.2	3 590	3.3	68	77	70	15	82	87	46
Uganda	200	3.1	320	4	40	41	218	185	14	8	48
UK	242	0.3	20 710	1.5	74	80	43	8	109	104	41

Figure 4.12 Selected data for a sample of countries

a Describe and explain what has happened to life expectancy.

b Why might the data on female participation in the labour force be unreliable?

c To what extent do the data support the view that development tends to favour men more than women?

d Which of the indicators do you think best reflects the level of development in a country? Give your reasons.

e To what extent is it possible to make judgements about levels of development from the sort of data provided in **4.11**? Justify your views.

A world in crisis

Countdown

The world is dying. What are you going to do about it?

Cover of *Sunday Times Magazine*, 26 February 1989

In many countries of the developed world, environmental issues moved to a high position on the political agenda in the late 1980s. There was a growing recognition that past forms of economic development had deleterious and potentially catastrophic effects on the natural environment. In the deluge of newspaper articles that accompanied this outpouring of concern for the environment were two assumptions: first, that the Earth is facing an ecological crisis of unheralded proportions and, second, that national governments must take action to prevent that crisis. While the late 1980s and early 1990s marked a heightened concern with environmental issues, it is important to recognise that such concerns have developed over a much longer time-span. Figure **5.1** takes up the chronology from the 1970s onwards.

Figure 5.1 Important dates in the rise of environmental concern

Date	Significant events
The 1970s 1973	The Convention on Trade in Endangered Species (CITES) signed – this concluded that trade is a major cause of species extinction. CITES banned trade in animal products such as tiger skins and turtle shells.
	The Trans-Amazon Highway completed – the road destroyed rainforests to provide access for loggers, ranchers and landless peasants.
	The Sahel drought – famine killed millions across a wide area of arid Africa. The process of desertification was recognised.
	The First Oil Crisis – OPEC imposed a huge rise in oil prices and brought postwar economic growth to a halt.
1978	The Love Canal – concerns about dioxin and related chemicals were heightened by the discovery of leaks in the basements of houses built on top of a chemical dump in the USA.

Date	Significant events
1979	The Three Mile Island accident – a major incident at a US nuclear power plant.

The Second Oil Crisis – another hike in oil prices. |
| *The 1980s*
1982 | The acid rain scandal in Europe – widespread tree deaths in Germany triggered by air pollution added to fears raised by fish deaths in acid streams and lakes in Scandinavia. |
1984	The Ethiopian famine – the second great famine in Africa in 10 years led to growing concern about climate change.
1985	The ozone hole – scientists in the Antarctic discovered a gaping 'hole' in the stratospheric ozone layer above the continent. The culprits were found to be chemicals, especially CFCs.
1986	Chernobyl – the world's largest nuclear disaster, with an expected final death toll of 10 000 – occurred at a nuclear power station in the Ukraine. Fallout reached the British Isles.
1987	The Montreal Protocol signed – international action taken to reduce the use of those chemicals most responsible for the growing ozone hole.
1988	North Sea seal deaths – a mysterious epidemic, thought to be caused by the build-up of poisonous organic chemicals, killed 18 000 seals.
1989	The *Exxon Valdez* – a tanker carrying crude oil from the Alaskan oilfields ran aground in Prince William Sound, releasing 12 million gallons of oil across a huge area of Arctic habitat.
The 1990s
1991	The Gulf War – deliberate destruction of oil wells ignited fires that burned for many months, unleashing huge clouds of black smoke across the region, causing lung diseases and polluting the desert with oil lakes.
1992	The ozone hole – now observed over the Arctic and seen as threatening heavily populated areas as far south as the UK. Fears were revived that the ultraviolet radiation streaming through the thinning ozone layer may be responsible for the rising incidence of skin cancer.
1994	The Desertification Convention was signed – there was growing concern about continuing environmental degradation of the dry lands of Africa.

Date	Significant events
	The Uruguay Round was concluded – the World Trade Organisation was set up, with powers to force countries to open their borders to free trade. This prompted fears that the environment would suffer as a result.
1997	Kyoto Protocol signed – industrial nations agreed to cut emissions of greenhouse gases by 5 per cent by 2010 as a practical step to reduce global warming.
1998	The millennium's hottest year.
	Borneo forest fires – landowners on this Indonesian island set huge areas of rainforest on fire as they cleared land for oil palm plantations (see **4.11**). The fires spread out of control in an unusually dry spell.
	El Niño – scientists said that the El Niño effect was intensifying and becoming more frequent. This is linked, according to some scientists, to global warming.

Review

1 Choose one of the events in **5.1**. Find out more about its causes, its effects and the way in which it influenced thinking about the environment.

2 Can you think of any more significant events, particularly since 1998, that you might add to **5.1**?

3 Compile a similar record for the beginning of the new millennium.

SECTION B

The relationship between resources and development

At the heart of debates about the relationship between people and the environment is the relationship between resources and development. The development of human societies depends on the physical resources that exist in the world. These resources act as raw materials and energy sources in industrial and agricultural processes. They absorb and transport the by-products of these processes. Resources are also consumed in the fulfilment of human needs for shelter and to sustain our lifestyles. It would seem to follow that limitations in the quantity and quality of resources will act as a barrier to development. The most famous version of this view of the relationship between resources and development was provided by Thomas

Malthus, who argued that there were fixed environmental limits to human development.

Malthus wrote *An Essay on the Principle of Population*, which was published in 1798. He argued that the limits to population growth would be determined by the supply of food. His argument was based on the claim that food production tended to increase in a simple arithmetic fashion (that is, 1, 2, 3, 4, 5 and so on), while population tended to increase in a geometric fashion (that is, 1, 2, 4, 8, 16, 32 and so on). Clearly, Malthus was suggesting that population growth would outstrip food production and that this would lead to famine and starvation. At a certain point, the limit of resources would be reached and the rate of population increase would level off. Up until that point, however, Malthus argued that there would be a tendency for population increase.

In order to understand why Malthus adopted such a pessimistic view, it is important to understand the context in which he was writing. This was a time of great change in English agriculture and industry. Many people were being displaced from the land by developments in agricultural technology, and seeking to find work in the rapidly growing towns and cities. Many wealthy people were worried that there was a 'surplus' of unnecessary workers. Malthus was seeking to understand this situation. Although Malthus was writing at the end of the 18th century, more recent writers have shared his pessimism. They are sometimes called **neo-Malthusians**, because they share Malthus' perspective that the size of the world's population is itself the cause of many problems. In his book *The Population Bomb* (1968), Paul Ehrlich wrote:

> *Each year food production in the undeveloped countries falls a bit further behind burgeoning population growth, and people go to bed a little bit hungrier.*

In 1972, in their report *The Limits to Growth*, the Club of Rome warned that the critical point in world population growth was approaching and that humanity needed to find a state of balance between population and resources. According to this view, rapid population growth is the main cause of the problems of the less-developed world since it leads to poverty, economic stagnation, environmental problems, rapid urbanisation, unemployment and political instability. Since rapid population growth is the cause of the problems, the solution is to persuade people to have fewer children – and the main way to achieve this is through family planning.

These ideas about the fixed limits of resources have been disputed. For instance, Karl Marx and Friedrich Engels argued that the population issue was a false one, and thought that the problem could be solved by new technological developments that would allow increased agricultural production and a more equal distribution of resources. More recently, the agricultural economist Ester Boserup (1965) argued that population growth was an important factor in allowing societies to find innovative ways to increase the stock of resources. This view suggests that, faced with new demands, people can adapt creatively to solve potential resource problems.

While the doomsday scenarios of the neo-Malthusians have not yet come true, and the idea that the Earth is facing extinction is less fashionable today, this does not mean that the relationship between human development and resources can be ignored. A moment's reflection will tell us that there are physical limits to the amounts of resources available. However, rather than focusing on the global picture, it may be more important to consider the relationship between particular groups of people in particular places or environments. Also, rather than focusing on the question of the overall level of resources available, it is important to ask questions about how resources are controlled, used and managed, since these matters may be as important as the physical amount of a resource.

Case study: Water resources

Water is fundamental to human existence and development. During the most intensive phase of economic development over the past century, global water withdrawals have increased sharply – and at rates that outstrip population growth. Total and per capita water consumption are generally higher in the developed world, and economic development leads to higher levels of use for industrial and domestic purposes. Worldwide, the consumption of water is doubling every 20 years. The International Water Management Institute has made projections of the water supply and demand for 118 countries over the period from 1990 to 2025 (**5.2**). They predict that 17 countries in the Middle East will all face 'absolute water scarcity' by 2025. These regions will not have enough water to maintain 1990 levels of per capita food production from irrigated agriculture and also to meet industrial and household needs.

The main cause of the water shortage is agriculture. Roughly 70 per cent of water diverted from rivers or drawn up from aquifers is used for irrigation. However, irrigation is a wasteful process, since leaking pipes, unlined channels, evaporation from reservoirs and canals, and poorly directed spraying means that two-thirds of the water never reaches the plants' roots. The result is that underground water supplies are being depleted, as farmers pump groundwater faster than precipitation can replenish it, causing a steady drop in the water table. The solution to the water supply crisis is a reduction in consumption, and one key area is to improve the efficiency of irrigation.

However, water resources are limited. The supply of water is dependent on the amount of rain that falls. Water has been described as the 'oil of the 1990s', which implies that it is essential for future economic development and for political stability. Indeed, the situation is perhaps more crucial since, unlike oil, there are no alternatives to replace water.

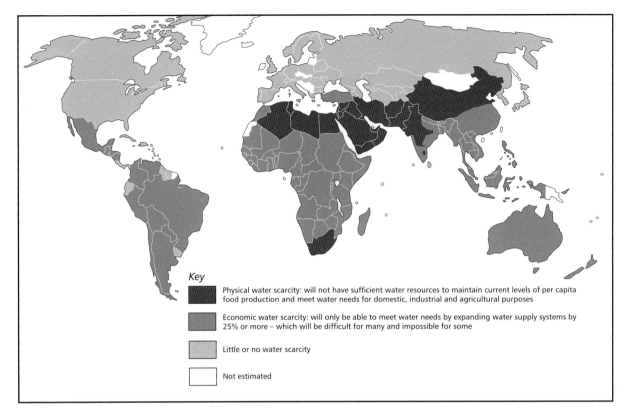

Key

Physical water scarcity: will not have sufficient water resources to maintain current levels of per capita food production and meet water needs for domestic, industrial and agricultural purposes

Economic water scarcity: will only be able to meet water needs by expanding water supply systems by 25% or more – which will be difficult for many and impossible for some

Little or no water scarcity

Not estimated

Figure 5.2 Projected water scarcity in 2025

Review

4 Summarise Malthus' view of population and resources. How relevant are his views today?

5 To what extent do you think that neo-Malthusian fears about the limits of resources are justified?

6 Identify the global pattern shown by **5.2**.

SECTION C

The global environmental challenge

In this section, some of the major global environmental challenges that have become the focus of concern over the past three decades are discussed.

Deforestation

Deforestation involves the removal of forests and woodlands through cutting or deliberate burning, at rates in excess of natural regeneration. It is notoriously difficult to gain accurate estimates of the rate at which deforestation is occurring. For instance, in 1982 the United Nation's Food

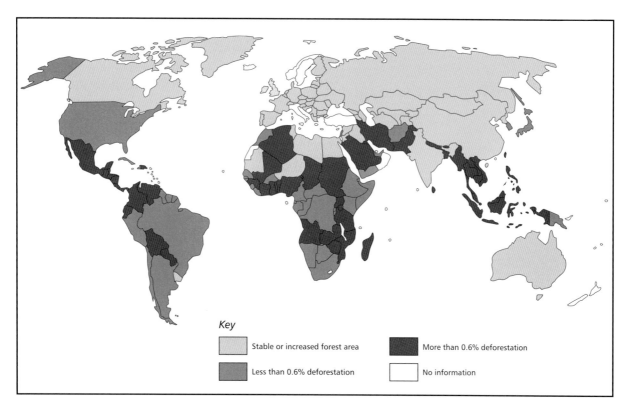

Key

Stable or increased forest area

More than 0.6% deforestation

Less than 0.6% deforestation

No information

Figure 5.3 Estimated annual rates of change in forest cover by country, 1981–1990

and Agricultural Organisation (FAO) estimated the rate of tropical forest loss to be around 114 000 km^2 per year (**5.3**). However, in 1990 the World Resources Institute reported that 204 000 km^2 were lost annually throughout the 1980s. Although deforestation is not a new phenomenon, it is the contemporary rates and extent of forest removal across the humid Tropics that are unprecedented and have led to global environmental concern in recent times.

Throughout the 1980s and 1990s, it was the deforestation of forests in the humid Tropics that generated most media and political concern. The exact causes of deforestation in the humid Tropics are unclear. Generally, those who cut down the trees fall into three groups: farmers, ranchers and loggers. The loss of forests is closely linked to the expansion of cropland, although the exact cause is not entirely clear. There are varying opinions:

■ some argue that the loss of forests is the outcome of government policies
■ others argue that it is due to small farmers, who have inadequate knowledge of the ecosystem requirements
■ yet others argue that it is linked to the penetration of capitalism and the modern debt crisis.

Figure **5.4** identifies the main causes of deforestation in different world regions.

Figure 5.4 The main causes of deforestation

Region	Main factors
Latin America	Cattle ranching, resettlement and spontaneous migration, agricultural expansion, road-building, population pressure, unequal social structure
Africa	Fuelwood collection, logging, agricultural expansion, population pressure
South Asia	Population pressure, agricultural expansion, political corruption, fodder collection, fuelwood collection
South-East Asia	Corruption, agricultural expansion, logging, population pressure

Case study: Deforestation in the Philippines

Forest cover in the Philippines declined from 70 per cent of the national land area to 50 per cent between 1900 and 1950 – and declined further, to below 25 per cent, in the early 1990s. The most common reason was that primary rainforest was converted to secondary forest by logging, and this secondary forest has then been cleared for the expansion of agriculture.

Figure 5.5 Factors affecting deforestation in the Philippines

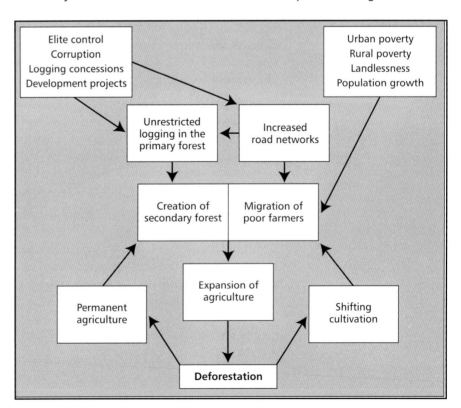

Figure **5.5** shows the complexity of the deforestation process. The granting of logging rights was linked to programmes of development, but also took the form of political favours to Filipino elites, in return for continued loyalty, and to foreign-based TNCs. In order to access their concession rights, these companies built roads into the forests. The process of logging exacerbated inequalities in the Philippines, and the urban and rural poor increasingly migrated to the forests in search of land. They cleared the secondary forests and sought to cultivate the land. This example indicates the difficulty of trying to understand the causes of deforestation.

Soil erosion and desertification

Soils form at slow rates – of a few millimetres per century – and their formation is controlled by factors such as geology, climate and topography. By contrast, soil erosion can be extremely rapid, perhaps several centimetres per year. The removal of tree cover exposes the soil surface to the direct impact of rainfall and also removes the effect of root binding on soil stability. Some commentators have argued that soil erosion, or land degradation, is the single most pressing global problem. Since 1945, an area roughly the size of China and India combined has been eroded to the point at which the land's ability to support agriculture has been impaired.

Soil erosion is one component of the wider processes of desertification. The causes of desertification are complex. It may be triggered by natural processes such as drought, or by the actions of wild animals that destroy vegetation. However, human actions may also lead to desertification, through population pressure that leads to overgrazing and deforestation. The over-use of pastures may result from allowing too many animals, or inappropriate types of animals, to graze. Intensive grazing causes two problems:

- ■ it can result in the removal of biomass
- ■ it can lead to trampling and compacting of the soil, which in turn leads to a decrease in vegetation cover and increased erosion by water or wind.

Increased grazing pressure can be caused by increased competition for land as cultivated areas are increased, pushing herders into more marginal pastures. This is true in many parts of the Sahel region of Africa, where expanding areas of sorghum and millet cultivation have led to a reduced range for nomadic pastoralists.

In discussing the causes of desertification, it is very easy to focus solely on the physical processes through which soil is degraded. In contrast, it can be argued that we need to look at the deeper, or structural, reasons why resources are misused. Figure **5.6** summarises some of the underlying explanations offered for land degradation.

Figure 5.6 Factors that encourage land degradation

Factor	Links to degradation
Natural disasters	Any resulting degradation is seen as inevitable, and as either an act of God or due to physical factors beyond human control
Population growth	This occurs when population growth exceeds the environmental carrying capacity
Underdevelopment	Resource exploitation for the benefit of developed countries, plus a lack of resource management, leads to over-use of the natural environment
The colonial legacy	Trade links, communications, cash crops and other 'hangovers' from the past have led to poor management of land resources
Inappropriate technology	The promotion of wrong strategies and techniques results in land degradation
Attitudes	These are linked to inappropriate technology and a lack of scientific knowledge, together with ignorance
War and civil unrest	The over-use of resources in national emergencies leads to high population pressure in safe locations; resources and the environment are damaged or destroyed

Global warming

One of the most important processes in the natural environment is the carbon cycle, within which oxygen emitted through processes of photosynthesis and respiration as carbon dioxide is circulated between the atmosphere, oceans and vegetation. The amount of carbon dioxide (CO_2) in the atmosphere determines the global surface temperature. The re-radiation of solar radiation back into space is controlled by the insulating effect of 'greenhouse gases' in the atmosphere. These gases include CO_2, methane and nitrous oxide. The average temperature of the Earth's surface has risen by approximately 0.5°C over the past 100 years, as concentrations of these greenhouse gases have built up in the atmosphere. This global warming has been proclaimed as the major environmental challenge facing humanity over the next century, but there is continued debate about the extent of global warming. There is a growing consensus amongst climatologists that the global average temperature is set to rise by 3°C over the next century.

The major source of carbon dioxide has been the burning of fossil fuels. Economic development has led to an increase in per capita consumption of coal, oil and natural gas. The production of this varies widely, between, for instance, the USA, which is the largest gross energy consumer, and many developing countries, where more than 90 per cent of total energy consumption is supplied by non-commercial sources. A second and increasingly important source of CO_2 is deforestation. The loss of tree cover reduces the uptake of CO_2 from the atmosphere and hence leads to higher levels of greenhouse gases. The subsequent burning of logs and biomass adds to the production of carbon through the oxidation process.

The major impacts of global warming include possible future sea-level rises (estimated at 5 mm per year in future, compared with the current rate of 1 mm), with the increased temperature leading to melting of mountain glaciers and ice-caps. Approximately 10 million people live less than 3 m above sea level.

The UN Framework on Climatic Change was signed by more than 150 countries at the Rio de Janeiro Earth Summit in 1992: it came into effect in 1994. The main point about the Convention is that the signatory countries committed themselves to reducing CO_2 emissions to 1990 levels. The Convention is limited by the fact that these commitments are voluntary. In 1997, the Kyoto Conference sought to make the commitments legally binding. The aim of the Kyoto Protocol is to cut the combined emission of greenhouse gases by about 5 per cent of their 1990 levels by 2008–2012, specifying the amount that each industrialised nation must contribute towards this overall aim. Those countries with the highest CO_2 emissions are expected to reduce their emissions by 6–8 per cent. The extent to which the aims of the Protocol can be realised remains to be seen. However, it is hard to imagine any government being willing to sacrifice economic growth in order to reduce CO_2 emissions. In the long term, the goal will be to achieve economic growth without consuming more and more fossil fuels. This may be achieved through improvements in the efficiency of fuel use or through the development of alternative renewable energy sources.

Urban atmospheric pollution

This may appear to be a local problem related to specific sources such as industry and transport, but is a global issue in the sense that all cities tend to experience similar problems. Sulphur dioxide (SO_2) is the most common urban pollutant, with most cities experiencing sulphurous smog at some point. An estimated 1 billion urban residents worldwide are exposed to levels of SO_2 in excess of World Health Organisation (WHO) guidelines. The sources of SO_2 are smelting of metallic ores, the burning of oil and coal for power production and heating, and transport exhaust emissions.

The health problems associated with SO_2 are mainly respiratory, which has the effect of putting increasing strain on the heart. In attempting to reduce the localised health risks, chimneys have been built higher to disperse emissions. However, this has had the effect of putting pollutants into the larger atmospheric circulation system for longer periods. The result has been acid deposition. In the 1980s this became a major issue, as drifting pollution from Europe was linked to the acidification of Scandinavian lakes and rivers. The results included damage to fish species and the disruption of soil nutrient cycles.

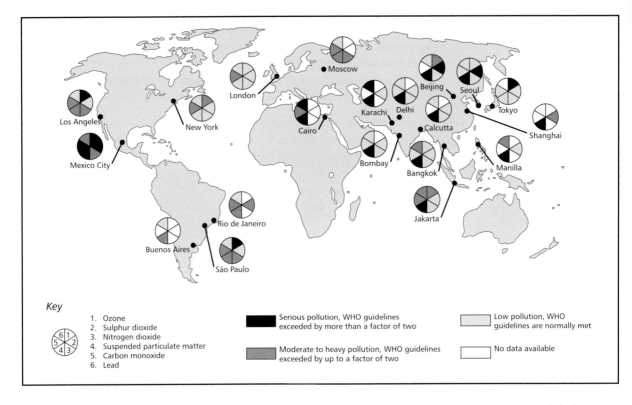

Figure 5.7 Air quality in 20 global mega-cities

Monitoring of urban air quality has been undertaken across a global network of mega-cities since 1974. The quality of air in 20 such cities is shown in **5.7**. There is clearly a distinction in urban air quality between cities in the developing and developed worlds. While cities in industrialised countries have made substantial reductions in air pollution during the past three decades, rapidly growing urban areas in developing countries pose serious pollution threats. Mexico City is the worst affected city, with WHO guidelines for SO_2 levels exceeded by a factor of two or more. The city's location exacerbates the problem of air pollution, since it lies in an elevated basin, surrounded by mountains, and experiences temperature inversions for, on average, 20 days per month from November to March. The result is that pollutants are trapped in the lower layers of the atmosphere and are not easily dispersed.

Loss of biodiversity

The first global assessment of biodiversity undertaken by the UNEP concluded that between 5 and 20 per cent of some groups of animal and plant species are threatened with extinction in the near future. The impacts of such losses are difficult to gauge, since scientific knowledge of ecosystems themselves is incomplete, and also because it is difficult to know the potential value of diversity in ecosystems, species and genetic materials.

The destruction of habitats is regarded as the greatest threat to biological diversity. In many countries, high population densities lead to the removal of natural habitat, to make space for farmland, settlement and industry. The main cause of loss of biodiversity is the intensification of agriculture. This includes eradication through the increased use of pesticides, the overcropping of animal species and the modification and loss of habitat through the encroachment of agriculture. For example, 85 per cent of the world's food supply is based on just 20 plant species.

It is the loss of habitats such as wetlands and forests that accounts for most of the loss of biodiversity. Tropical forests are especially species rich. Although only occupying just 7 per cent of the Earth's surface, they account for between 50 and 90 per cent of all known plant and animal species.

Another cause of biodiversity loss is exploitation of animals through hunting. It is probably true that the loss of species has been occurring since the Stone Age. However, the advent of guns gave people the power to exterminate creatures in large numbers, a notable example being the eradication of the buffalo in North America. Today, hunters kill migrating birds in large numbers. Large mammals are also hunted: their products fetch high prices in the local and international markets. The African elephant population was reduced by half in the 1980s, from 1.3 million to 600 000, before a ban on ivory trading was introduced in 1989.

In recent decades, there has been heightened awareness of the issue of biodiversity loss and there have been a number of efforts to reduce it. There have been a number of international agreements. Some, such as the Ramsar Convention for Wetlands, have focused on specific habitats. Others, such as the CITES agreement, have focused on international trade. The Convention on Biological Diversity was designed to ensure the conservation of biological resources and their sustainable use, and to promote a fair share of the benefits arising from genetic resources.

Case study: The case against biodiversity

Moore, Chaloner and Stott challenge the idea that maintaining biodiversity is crucial to human life on Earth. They point out that the issue of biodiversity is used to make the case for keeping rainforests completely undisturbed or for sustainable use.

Against this, they argue that research shows that the genetic resources that remain when forests are cleared tend to be more highly valued by the local populations. They give the example of Benin in West Africa. Farmers clear their forests for fields, and on average retain 63 trees per hectare, which are used to produce the vegetable oils employed in cooking and soap-making. These resources could be obtained without clearing the forest, but it is much easier to exploit them in the fields and it makes sense for farmers to do so. In addition, the traditional sources are now being replaced by the production of groundnut oil and soybean. They say that change is taking place, and new resources being exploited, in the search for an easier and more profitable life. To argue that these farmers should not clear the forests has the effect of holding back their competitive development and condemning the farmers to an extremely hard life.

Moore, Chaloner and Stott do not deny that some of the Earth's biodiversity will be of use to people, but point out that 99.99 per cent of all life that has ever existed on the surface of the Earth has become extinct, from the trilobites through dinosaurs to mammoths. They argue that extinction is a normal process of change, which does not result in the destruction of the Earth:

> Humans do not have an absolute interest in 'all' biodiversity, only that biodiversity which is perceived to be of value to Homo sapiens and to the survival of H. sapiens, such as new crops, drug plants, pretty flowers, and cuddly animals. By stark contrast, potential enemies, like viruses, bacteria, and even some insect, bird and mammal pests and disease vectors, should, of course, be eradicated at all costs. There is nothing intrinsically wrong in arguing the case for maintaining selected species, so long as we are honest about it: we are doing so because these species are thought to be useful to us or because we like them.

What they are saying here is that we need to think carefully about the values that we put on animals and environments. Part of the problem with the biodiversity argument is that it involves imposing Northern values about the environment upon people in the developing world, who may make very different assessments about the values of certain plants and animal species.

Case study: China and the challenge of sustainable development

From 1949 to 1976, China followed a path of socialist industrialisation. This entailed developing its own industries in order to become economically self-sufficient. The key to success was increased production. However, the results of these policies included a series of environmental problems, as pollution and over-use of resources were considered less important than meeting the needs of a rapidly increasing population. Since 1976, after the death of China's leader Mao Zedong, China has gradually sought to integrate itself into the world capitalist economy. In the light of this partial conversion to capitalism, many commentators predict that China will become a major source of goods and services, and

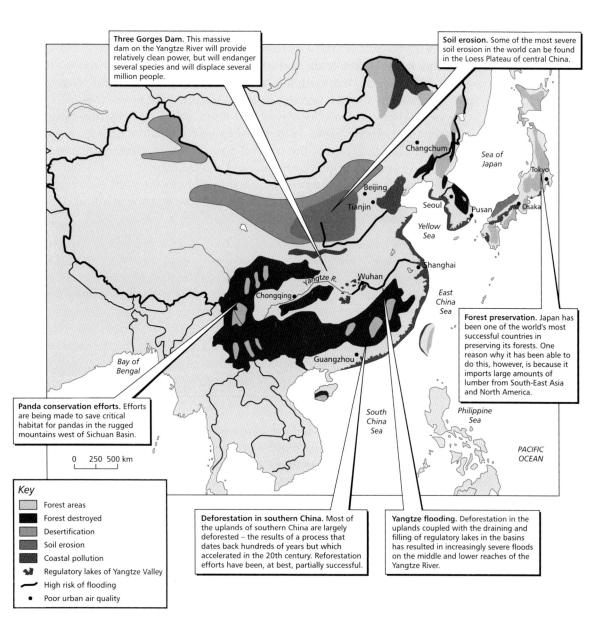

Three Gorges Dam. This massive dam on the Yangtze River will provide relatively clean power, but will endanger several species and will displace several million people.

Soil erosion. Some of the most severe soil erosion in the world can be found in the Loess Plateau of central China.

Forest preservation. Japan has been one of the world's most successful countries in preserving its forests. One reason why it has been able to do this, however, is because it imports large amounts of lumber from South-East Asia and North America.

Panda conservation efforts. Efforts are being made to save critical habitat for pandas in the rugged mountains west of Sichuan Basin.

Deforestation in southern China. Most of the uplands of southern China are largely deforested – the results of a process that dates back hundreds of years but which accelerated in the 20th century. Reforestation efforts have been, at best, partially successful.

Yangtze flooding. Deforestation in the uplands coupled with the draining and filling of regulatory lakes in the basins has resulted in increasingly severe floods on the middle and lower reaches of the Yangtze River.

Changchum
Sea of Japan
Tokyo
Beijing
Tianjin
Seoul
Pusan
Osaka
Yellow Sea
Shanghai
Yangtze R.
Wuhan
Chongqing
East China Sea
Bay of Bengal
Guangzhou
South China Sea
Philippine Sea
PACIFIC OCEAN

0   250 500 km

Key

- Forest areas
- Forest destroyed
- Desertification
- Soil erosion
- Coastal pollution
- Regulatory lakes of Yangtze Valley
- High risk of flooding
- Poor urban air quality

Figure 5.8 Environmental issues in East Asia

the largest market for consumer goods. Environmentalists are concerned that rapid economic development for China will have grave environmental consequences, unless development is planned to sustain the environment and resources. Figure **5.8** shows some of the major environmental issues in the region.

As the result of centuries of clearance for fuelwood and for crop growing, most of the uplands of southern China are largely deforested. Attempts have been made to reforest, but these have been only partially successful. China suffers a shortage of forest resources. Continued economic growth will lead to a huge demand for timber, pulp and paper in the future.

Soil erosion is a major problem, especially on the loess plateau of central China. Loess is a fine, wind-blown material, deposited during the last ice age. It forms fertile soil, but is easily washed away when exposed to running water. The natural vegetation of tough grasses and scrub was removed by farmers seeking to grow crops on the fertile soils. As population gradually increased, the result was ever increasing rates of soil loss, which caused deep gullies to be cut into the hillside. Today, the loess plateau is one of the poorest parts of China. Good farmland is limited and drought is common, and the problem is exacerbated by the continued expansion of the population. The government encourages farmers to build terraces to conserve the soil, and the planting of woody vegetation to bind the soil.

As China industrialises, the demand for power is increasing. Currently, this demand is met by burning low-quality coal, which is plentiful but results in serious pollution. Smog is a problem in cities in the winter months, when stagnant air masses sit over central and southern China. In addition, coal-burning is leading to problems of acid rain. One solution to this has been to build dams, such as the Three Gorges Dam. However, while this may reduce air pollution it will not satisfy the demand for energy, and environmentalists are critical of dams, since they lead to the displacement of people and the destruction of habitats.

This chapter has provided a brief introduction to some of the major environmental problems that have grabbed the headlines in the past three decades. As was suggested in **Chapter 2**, the process of globalisation has led to the development of a global environmental consciousness. People are increasingly aware of the interdependency of people and the natural environment at a global scale. One of the problems of reading a chapter such as this is that it is easy to become overwhelmed by the scale of the problems, so that we end up with a picture of doom and gloom – the doomsday scenario. In **Chapter 6**, we consider the idea that future forms of development will need to take into account the natural environment and the idea of sustainable development.

Review

7 Define **desertification**.

8 Distinguish between the physical and structural causes of desertification.

9 Attempt to rank the causes of land degradation in **5.6** according to their importance. For each cause, suggest what would have to be done in order to reduce its impact.

10 Explain how global warming is related to human activity.

11 What measures are being taken to reduce global warming?

12 Write a short analytical account of the information shown in **5.7**.

13 Explain what is meant by **biodiversity**, and why it is considered to be an important global issue.

14 Summarise the case against biodiversity presented on page 81.

15 Draw a sketch map of China. Annotate it to show the major environmental challenges facing the country.

Enquiry

1 Global warming is widely believed to be occurring now. Undertake some research, using CD-ROMs, the Internet and other sources, to learn about:

■ deforestation in one global region, particularly its causes and any measures being taken to control it
■ the debate surrounding global warming.

2 Study **5.9** and explain three ways in which drought could lead to land degradation.

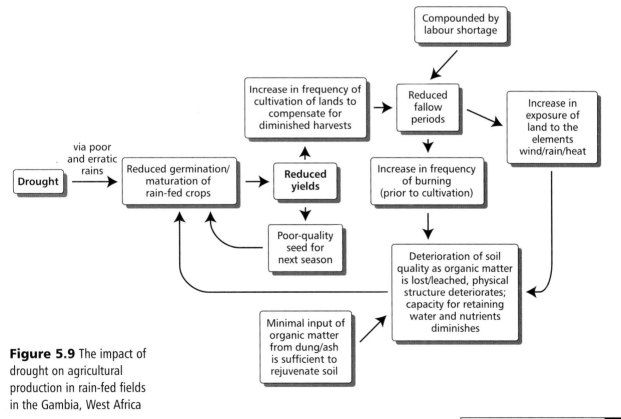

Figure 5.9 The impact of drought on agricultural production in rain-fed fields in the Gambia, West Africa

Sustainable development – a sustainable idea?

In earlier chapters, we have looked at theories of development, the idea of globalisation, differences in the economic development of regions and the environmental issues raised by patterns of development and globalisation. The approach adopted has been a critical one. What this means is that the discussions have sought to dig beneath the surface and provide deeper explanations to understand the shape of the world. As in any account, the explanations and theories offered are partial, in the sense that they only tell part of the whole story, and that the author clearly has his own position in relation to the issues. You may have guessed, for instance, that the author is sceptical about the concept of development and the idea that, currently, globalisation is leading to an improved quality of life for the majority of the world's people.

In this final chapter, the concept of sustainability is explored, and then the idea that sustainable development can offer a solution to current economic and environmental problems is critically examined.

SECTION A

What is sustainability?

It has been suggested that there are more than 70 definitions of sustainable development in current use. The current use of the term derives from a series of important reports in the 1980s and early 1990s, which argue that human societies need to move towards a form of sustainable development. Put simply, sustainable development is a form of development that combines economic production and the satisfaction of human needs with the capacity of the environment to cope with the consequences of economic activity. So far so good. However, as this chapter seeks to show, what exactly this means and how it can be achieved are matters that are open to debate and interpretation.

The concept of sustainability first emerged at the UN Conference on the Human Environment, held in Stockholm in 1972. The conference itself was marked by a division between the developed and developing countries. The developing countries regarded the developed countries' concerns about the effects of pollution and technology on the environment as the worries of a wealthy and exclusive club. The developing countries were more worried that such environmental concerns might act as a barrier to their own attempts to industrialise. The concept of sustainable development was coined as an attempt to suggest that an option existed for development that would allow rapid economic growth without environmental damage.

Since the Stockholm Conference, the concept has evolved and is now used in a variety of ways by groups with different interests. One example is that of the World Conservation Strategy in 1980, which used the term to argue for conservation. The World Conservation Strategy had the following objectives:

- to maintain essential ecological processes and life support systems
- to preserve genetic diversity
- to ensure the sustainable use of species and ecosystems.

In this definition of sustainable development, the focus was on the environment or ecological concerns. This use of the term 'sustainable development' was taken on board by the World Commission on Environment and Development in 1986. *Our Common Future*, otherwise known as the Brundtland Report, took a different view of the concept. It shifted the focus away from the environment, towards the economic and political context in which development occurs. It suggested that environmental issues could not be separated from basic development needs, since environmental degradation was often the result of the poverty that drives people to overgraze or cut down forests in order to meet their basic needs. The Brundtland Report argued that the way forward was through co-operation between rich and poor countries in the context of development. This would lead to sustainability through careful economic growth.

The Brundtland Report led directly to the UN Conference on Environment and Development (UNCED) in 1992. The UN General Assembly debated the Brundtland Report and it was decided to hold this conference. It was held in Rio de Janeiro in Brazil, and is often referred to as the 'Earth Summit'. It was the promise of 'green' growth that persuaded both rich and poor countries to come to the negotiating table.

Adams (1995) argues that though there has been much excitement about the concept of sustainable development, little of the discussion has been about development. This is because the concept has its roots in another set of debates, namely those concerned with 'environmentalism'. This begins to explain the important changes that took place in the debate during the short period of time between the publication of the Brundtland Report in 1986 and the Earth Summit in 1992. The central point made in the Brundtland Report was that as long as there is acute poverty, then there would inevitably be environmental degradation. In its own words, 'a world in which poverty and inequality are endemic will always be prone to ecological and other crises'. The report suggested that the solution was a revival of economic growth, but with an important difference with regard to the quality of the growth. The report went on to call for basic needs to be met, for populations to be stabilised, for resources to be conserved and for technology to be put to better use.

However, the Earth Summit turned away from this approach and instead shifted the focus to a number of pressing environmental problems, thus moving the debate away from development and towards the environment. The matters debated at Rio and reflected in the discussions afterwards were:

- climate change resulting from the enhanced greenhouse effect
- the depleted ozone layer
- polluted and over-fished seas
- desertification
- the growing shortage of fresh water
- the loss of biodiversity.

These are obviously issues of huge importance, but critics have suggested that this is an exercise in cynicism on the part of the developed countries, since it suggests that these are global problems that are globally produced. This ignores the argument that it is the industry of the developed countries that is largely responsible for these environmental problems, yet it is the countries of the developing world that are being asked to pay for their solution. This explains much of the argument and discussion at the Rio Earth Summit. The developing countries had a very different perspective, seeing poverty and the environmental problems associated with it as the main issues. The two worlds also disagreed over what actions should be taken and who should pay for them. Developing countries feared that their development would stifled by restrictive agreements on atmospheric emissions, and were keen to defend their right to use the natural resources, such as tropical forests, within their boundaries for development without restrictions by environmentalists in the developed world.

Review

1 Attempt to define **sustainable development**.

2 Why do you think that there are over 70 different definitions of sustainable development in current use?

3 Outline the significance of the following events in terms of sustainable development:

- the Stockholm Conference of 1972
- the Brundtland Report of 1986
- the Rio Earth Summit in 1992.

The contested nature of sustainable development

As with the concepts of development and globalisation, what appears to be a concept that we can all agree upon turns out to be much more complicated and debatable than previously imagined. This is because sustainable development is an inherently political concept. What needs to be done to secure the livelihoods of people – and yet at the same time protect the environment – is open to debate and argument. Figure **6.1** summarises some of the main Western schools of thought about the environment. Some of the terms may be unfamiliar to you, since they are inevitably based on political concepts. What **6.1** indicates is the wide variety of ideas about the environment and sustainability, which suggests that it is premature to attempt to define, once and for all, what sustainable development is.

Figure 6.1 Different views of sustainability and the environment

School of thought	Main features
Cornucopian	Any problems are capable of solution through human ingenuity
Market-based	An emphasis on the market mechanism will resolve environmental concerns
Managerialist	Environmental problems result from poor organisation and decision-making – more rational structures can resolve these problems
Reformist	Sustainable development should be promoted through the integration of environmental policy with economic development – there is a need to reduce global disparities through changes in trade policies
Post-industrialist	The ideology of individualism is the underlying problem – the focus should be on changing individual attitudes
Limits to growth	It is necessary to control both population and economic growth
Deep ecologist	Wilderness areas should be preserved and the intrinsic values of nature should be respected
Communitarian	Society should be transformed into numerous decentralised and largely self-sufficient communities
Marxist	Environmental problems are an inevitable consequence of capitalism – a socialist society is needed
Eco-feminist	The domination and destruction of nature is the consequence of a patriarchal society

Broadly speaking, the schools of thought represented in **6.1** can be divided into two groups: those that are 'technocentric' and those that are 'ecocentric'.

Technocentric views of sustainable development

Technocentrism is based on the belief that humans are able to manage nature comfortably, and even to improve it. Examples would include the idea that the flooding of rivers can be controlled through engineering schemes, or that food production can be improved and increased through genetic modification of plants. Environmental problems are technical matters that can be resolved through technology, the economy and better management. In **6.1**, the Cornucopian, market-based and managerialist approaches are all examples of technocentric views of the environment. Cornucopians believe that the physical environment and resources are there to be used to fuel economic growth. They have faith in the power of human creativity to solve any environmental problems. The market-based approach shares this optimism, but places the emphasis on the importance of economic mechanisms to overcome environmental problems. For example, firms that pollute the environment will end up with higher economic costs in the long term, and will therefore find that it is more profitable to use environmental resources carefully.

Ecocentric views of sustainable development

Ecocentrism is based on a different set of beliefs about the relationship between people and the environment. Ecocentrists assume that environmental issues have more to do with our ethical and moral approaches to nature than to technical difficulties and their solution. They suggest that we need to make fundamental changes to our relationship with nature. Again, there is a wide variety of approaches. For instance, the Deep ecologists advocate a minimum use of the physical environment and its resources, stressing nature's intrinsic value and the rights of non-human species. On the other hand, communitarians propose the need to develop small-scale communities that are more in tune with nature and are based on values of co-operation and sharing, with power shared at a local level. Eco-feminists argue that mainstream approaches to the environment are dominated by masculine values of greed and competitiveness, and they argue for a fundamental change in the use of the environment.

How should we understand current concerns with sustainability? In one sense, the concern is part of an understanding that the forms of development now being followed by many nations are destructive of the environment. To go back to the theories of development discussed in **Chapter 1**, it might be argued that sustainable development is an attempt to make modernisation theory face up to the fact that Western models of development have led to the destruction of the environment. For development theory as produced in the developed countries, the question is posed as whether economic goals can be reconciled with environmental goals. It is worth pointing out that mainstream discussions about sustainable development share many of the features of development theory as outlined in **Chapter 1**.

First, in mainstream thinking about sustainable development, economic growth remains at the centre. Other dimensions of development are treated as obstacles or potential barriers to economic growth. So the issue is framed in terms of how to overcome the 'problem' of the environment. Second, proper management is seen as the key to sustainable growth. This is already available in the developed countries, so it is simply a matter of accounting for the environment in economic transactions. Science and technology hold the key to overcoming the barriers to development presented by the environment. It is argued that developing countries should follow the lead of the developed countries in order to achieve sustainable development.

From the perspective of political and economic elites in the developing countries, however, sustainable development reflects the double standards of the developed nations. They ruined their own environments in the process of development, and are now asking others to restrict their own economic processes of wealth creation. Yet many people in the developing countries see wealth as a cause of, not a solution to, environmental crises. Post-development theorists would point out that the vast majority of people in the world already have lifestyles that do not put much pressure on ecosystems, and do not engage in wasteful consumerist practices. From their point of view, sustainable development is just another example of an attempt by so-called developed nations to impose their way of thinking and acting on local people.

These observations suggest that any discussions of future sustainability need to recognise the different histories of environmental use of different regions. For instance, it might be suggested that:

- the countries of the developed world need to focus on repairing the environmental damage caused by their long history of overconsumption
- the former communist countries of Eastern Europe need to focus on the modernisation of wasteful and polluting technologies that have led to heavily polluted environments
- the countries of the developing world need to focus on stabilising population growth in order to reduce pressure on resources.

Figure **6.2** is an attempt to develop the idea that different regions have different roles to play in realising global sustainability:

- Low-income, low-density regions, such as Amazonia and Malaya–Borneo, include the world's remaining settlement frontiers. These have only experienced large-scale clearance for agriculture, grazing and timber in recent decades. Before this, they were characterised by shifting cultivation, small-scale plantations and mining sites. However, the fact that much of the current clearance is being undertaken by poor farmers, and the lack of institutions to manage this clearance, means that sustainable development in these areas will be difficult to attain.

Figure 6.2 A schematic classification of some major world regions, based on population density and relative affluence

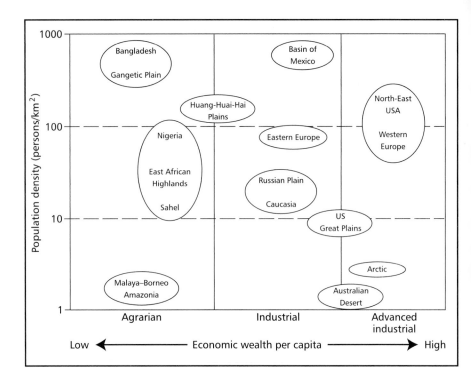

- Low-income, high-density regions, such as the Ganges–Brahmaputra floodplains and the northern plains of China, have long histories of subsistence agriculture. In recent decades this has been accompanied by rapid industrial development and urbanisation, resulting in pollution problems. The main challenge in such regions is to manage the movement of people from agriculture to industry, and the associated rural to urban migration that is taking place.
- Developing world countries, such as the Basin of Mexico, have a history of agriculture, but have experienced rapid population growth and industrialisation. There are problems of congestion and pollution in the primate cities. There is a need for policies of national decentralisation to manage these pressures.
- Densely populated, wealthy and industrialised regions have had a disproportionate impact on the environment. These impacts have been at local, continental and global levels – through, for example, acid rain and greenhouse gas emissions. In recent decades, these regions have achieved some success in improving environmental quality, albeit at a local scale.

4 Which of the schools of thought in **6.1** impresses you most? Justify your choice.

5 Distinguish between ecocentric and technocentric views of sustainable development.

6 Look at a selection of A-level textbooks that discuss sustainable development. Do they tend to adopt an ecocentric or a technocentric view?

7 Which of the two views of sustainable development do you prefer? Give your reasons.

8 Explain the significance of **6.2**.

SECTION C

Conclusions

The three words that make up the title of this book – development, globalisation and sustainability – are all interconnected (**6.3**). For instance, the idea that any nation can undergo development without reference to its position in a world in which goods and people are on the move is increasingly difficult to sustain (if it was ever possible). Similarly, notions of national boundaries are increasingly redundant in a world in which environmental goods and ills spread over wide geographical areas. Globalisation has a number of important implications for thinking about the contemporary world:

■ events in one part of the world may have profound implications for others
■ the idea of territorial space has become problematic, as flows of people, money and ideas challenge the ability of governments to control these movements
■ globalisation is producing a more unequal and hierarchical world, in which some people and places are better able than others to take advantage of new opportunities for movement and travel
■ the distinction between the 'global' and the 'local' is harder to sustain.

Figure 6.3 Links between development, globalisation and sustainability

There is an increasing disparity between the rich and the poor, between those countries and regions that already have wealth (and are getting richer through globalisation), and those that do not. These disparities in wealth are leading to greater variations in the levels of health care and education amongst the world's population.

There is a tension between the increased cultural homogeneity resulting from globalisation and the re-emergence of local movements of cultural and ethnic identity. The question of how to live with difference is becoming increasingly urgent.

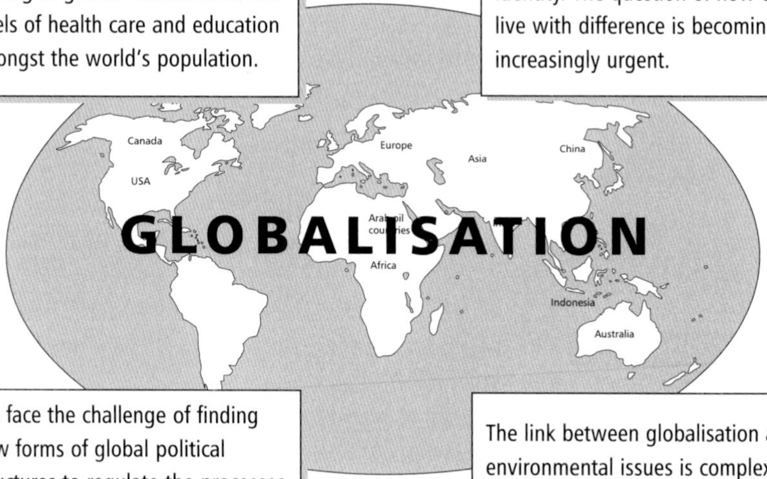

GLOBALISATION

Canada

USA

Europe

Asia

China

Arab oil countries

Africa

Indonesia

Australia

We face the challenge of finding new forms of global political structures to regulate the processes of globalisation. According to some, the nation–state is being undermined by global processes. As recent climate talks indicate, it is not easy to reach agreement on how to approach global issues.

The link between globalisation and environmental issues is complex. On the one hand, it argued that the world's nation–states are willing to sign international agreements to solve environmental problems (for example, treaties on whaling ocean pollution). On the other hand, it is argued that globalisation has aggravated environmental problems by promoting free trade.

These are important issues for geographers to address, and this book has been written to help you think about them and, hopefully, to encourage you to find out more about them. It does not claim to have all the answers: rather, the hope is to provoke you into making up your own mind about how the shape of the world is changing. The resources suggested at the end of the book will help you to take your thinking further.

Further reading and resources

The best place to keep abreast of developments in the world economy is through newspapers and magazines, such as *The Financial Times* (especially its periodic national surveys), *The Economist* and *The Guardian*. *The New Internationalist* is published monthly and provides a critical view of the impacts of globalisation on people and environments. As you use these resources, try to ask yourself which view of globalisation and development they tend to favour.

The annual *Human Development Report* provides a perspective on the impacts of globalisation and is a source of up-to-date statistics.

The Internet can be useful source of information, although – as with all sources – you need to ask some critical questions about who has decided to make material available, and why.

In terms of books, a good place to start is with standard AS- and A-level textbooks. In addition, the following sources develop some of the arguments made in this book:

R. Potter *et al.*, *Geographies of Development* (Longman, 1999) provides a good overview of thinking about development.

Jan Aaart Sholte, *Globalization: a Critical Introduction* (Macmillan, 2000) provides a useful summary of debates about globalisation in a range of academic subjects.

Paul Knox and John Agnew, *The Geography of the World Economy* (Arnold, 1994) is a useful textbook that provides a broader perspective on the development of the global economy.

Peter Dicken, *Global Shift* (Paul Chapman, 1998) is the standard text on recent changes in the nature of the global economy.

Michael Barrett Brown, *Global Crisis* (Spokesman, 1999) is written with sixth-form students in mind and takes a reformist view of globalisation.

Naomi Klein, *No Logo: no Space, no Choice, no Jobs* (Flamingo, 2001). This book, written from a more radical perspective, provides much detail on the operations of TNCs and the grassroots resistance to them.

N. Middleton, *The Global Casino* (Arnold, 2000) deals with the environmental issues discussed in this book.

A. Dobson, *Green Political Thought* (Routledge, 1990) is a readable introduction to environmental politics.

K. Dodds, *Geopolitics in a Changing World* (Prentice-Hall, 2000) is a readable introduction to the political debates associated with globalisation, development and sustainability.

J. Seager, *Earth Follies* (Earthscan, 1993). The subtitle of this book is 'Coming to feminist terms with the global environmental crisis'. It provides some thought-provoking material.